West Philadelphia Seventh-day Adventist Church
4527 Haverford Avenue
Philadelphia, PA 19139
Tel: 215-222-5707

set
Free

ENDORSEMENTS

"We are living in the most thrilling time in history. Despite troubles throughout the world, genuine works of God are springing up. Unstoppable works. Roy Peterson and American Bible Society are a big part of what God is doing. I've come to know Roy as a creative, global visionary. I've seen his enduring commitment. He is making it possible for God's healing Word to be available to hundreds of millions in their mother tongue. In this book Roy brings us up close and personal, showing how he began to apply God's Word in his own life. He weaves that story together with gripping adventures of the Bible transforming nations, in jungles and cities worldwide. If you want to be part of finishing the Great Commission of Jesus, you must read this. You're going to like it."

LOREN CUNNINGHAM
Founder, Youth With A Mission

"Focus, priority, and trust. These words reverberate inspiration and reflection through Roy's passionate writing. *Set Free* contains authentic and tangible fingerprints of God's work in and through lives of ordinary individuals in America and around the world. Roy Peterson wrote so convincingly that God can use yielded vessels from any background and any past; transforming them into testimonies of His grace and glory. The power of the Word of God to set free, to give purpose, and to cultivate true love is a transcultural phenomenon. This book will inspire you to reflect, to focus, and to take action now."

DANIEL LIM
CEO, International House of Prayer

"When we hear from God, we are transformed. Roy Peterson embodies this truth, both in the way he lives and the groundbreaking work he's empowering to make sure everyone can experience Scripture in their heart language. With a servant heart and strategic mind, Roy serves a critical role in propelling us toward the realization of a generations-old dream—seeing the Bible translated into every language. We have the potential to see this happen in our lifetime, thanks in part to the vision and passion of people like Roy. I've learned a great deal in working with him, and am thankful for this book so that many others can be inspired by Roy's story."

BOBBY GRUENEWALD
Pastor, Innovation Leader at Life.Church

"Dr. Roy Peterson is living proof that the Bible transforms lives. In sharing his own story and the stories of others who have experienced God's grace through His Word, Dr. Peterson offers a comfort to those searching for God's presence. *Set Free* is an encouragement for all of us to pursue God and be pursued by Him in the Scriptures."

BOB CRESON
President/CEO, Wycliffe Bible Translators USA

"God consistently breaks our preconceived patterns! Dr. Peterson's life trajectory was interrupted by God time and again. His love for Scripture and his responses to the Living Word are so utterly clear that God has chosen to place him in the leadership role in a unique institution. If one life can be changed, can God not change 100 million lives who are engaged to the Holy Word?"

SAMUEL E. CHIANG
President and Chief Executive Officer, Seed Company

"This book chronicles my friend Roy Peterson's personal journey of discovery that there are nearly 7,000 languages spoken on the planet and God speaks every one of them! Roy's engaging story shows how God delights in using ordinary broken people for His Kingdom purposes. I loved reading how he knew God was at work in him when an upcoming missions conference was more exciting to him than making a $5 million business deal. Fresh vision and new directions have developed in the entire Bible translation movement because of Roy's passion for God's Word and lost people. I love Roy Peterson and the ministries he has served. Let this book sweep you along and make you part of one of the greatest joy-filled movements in all human history. . . . getting God's Word into the heart language of every people group!"

RANDY ALCORN
Author of *Heaven, Happiness* and *The Treasure Principle*

"I met Roy Peterson almost 10 years ago and was captured by three things I saw in him: strong leadership, true humility and a zeal for God's Word and the souls of men and women. . .okay. . .maybe that's four things. *Set Free* isn't really a book about the life of Roy and Rita Peterson; it is a book about a God who delights in using people whose hearts are fully committed to Him. If you want to be encouraged by a tremendous story and challenged to take seriously the Great Commission and the vital role God's Word plays in its completion, then this is a must-read book for you."

DAVID WILLS
President, National Christian Foundation

"I count Roy a dear friend and have known him for nearly 15 years. Along the way I've seen his courageous, visionary leadership of multiple agencies pave the way for millions upon millions of people around the world to have an encounter with God through the Bible. I am also fully confident that the release of this excellent book will enable that to happen for many millions more all the way to the ends of the earth as God's Word accomplishes its purpose in their lives."

J TODD PETERSON
NFL 1994-2006 Chairman, Pro Athletes Outreach
Chairman Emeritus, Seed Company

"Our great and sovereign God carries out His divine plan for humanity through the lives of ordinary Christians who surrender themselves to trust and follow Him. Dr. Peterson's life is a clear and beautiful illustration of this truth. In this honest reflection on the events of his life, Roy demonstrates how God uses those who love Him—sometimes in very unexpected ways—to spread the life-saving message of the gospel. His journey shows us that we don't have to be perfect to be used by God, and we don't have to know what the future holds. We just have to have enough courage and patience to continue taking each next step forward. Countless lives have been blessed over the years by Roy's willingness to simply place himself in God's hands, and many more will be blessed by the testimony he offers in these pages."

THE REVEREND LUIS CORTÉS, JR.
President/CEO, Esperanza

"The Word of God has a power all its own, but it spreads by personal witness. *Set Free* is Roy Peterson's vivid and engaging witness to the Bible's liberating impact on his own life, and the transformative power of the Bible movement in the lives of millions of others. This is a wonderful, deeply enriching read."

CHARLES J. CHAPUT
O.F.M. Cap., Archbishop of Philadelphia

"There is no effort in our time of greater importance than the Bible movement. *Set Free* by Dr. Roy L. Peterson will challenge believers of all traditions to engage with the Scriptures. Most important, it is a reminder that we—you and I—have a divine mandate to be participants, not spectators, to impact and influence people with the Word of God. Your life will be changed by reading this book and you will be moved to ask, 'Lord, what can I do?'"

TESSIE GÜELL DEVORE
Publisher & Executive Vice President, Charisma House

"Dr. Peterson's life story is a poignant reminder that God's Word is powerful enough to capture the heart of a man in a Mexican prison and transform him to the point of one day manning the helm of world-renowned Wycliffe Bible Translators and now President & CEO of the American Bible Society proliferating Scripture in the United States and around the world. His unexpected journey has always been fueled by the belief that God's Word changes lives. Hence his unbridled passion and commitment to remove the barriers of language to ensure that everyone—no matter what tribe, nation or tongue—has the ability to experience the Gospel and undergo a radical life transformation. Everyone needs to read Dr. Peterson's larger-than-life story and be reminded that engaging in Scripture is the only thing that has the power to change lives and fulfill destinies."

ROB HOSKINS
President, OneHope, Inc.

ROY PETERSON

with BEN STROUP

Set

UNSTOPPABLE *HOPE*
FOR A WORLD THAT IS WAITING

Free

AMERICAN
BIBLE
SOCIETY

NEW YORK

For every partner in the work of Bible mission who has
relentlessly refused to leave the world waiting for hope, for all
those I am grateful to call partners, colleagues and friends.

And to my wife, Rita, who through every season,
over so many years,
has made me realize just how remarkably blessed I am.

TABLE OF CONTENTS

FOREWORD

MART GREEN

On February 5, 1998, I found my nerves on edge as I flew to Guatemala from Oklahoma. I was on my way to a small town, flying to be with the Eastern Jacaltec, or Potpo', people of Guatemala for the dedication of their New Testament. My distracted state of mind had nothing to do with the long plane ride and everything to do with what I was reading.

I was learning about these people. At the time, there were 30,000 of them living in the country, 1,000 of whom were believers. Of those, 400 could read. What was troubling my thoughts at that moment was that our family had just spent $20,000 to print the Eastern Jacaltec New Testaments—but only 400 people could read it!

"Why in the world did I not figure this out before I sent the money? Would this be considered a good return on an investment?" I asked myself, replying with what seemed to me the obvious answer: "I don't think so."

The next morning I got on a bus for an eight-hour, winding, up-down-and-around journey to the Eastern Jacaltec region. The all-day bus ride gave me time to stew even more over the thought, "Was this a good return on investment to spend so much money for such a small group of people?"

As the sun rose on the morning of February 7, we joined in the parade that was going through the town. It was a big day for the Eastern Jacaltec. Their Bible translation had started decades before—in 1958. They had waited forty years for this day!

During the dedication service, leaders from the community ceremoniously gave a Bible to each translator who had worked all those years, getting God's Word into their heart language. When Gaspar, who had been with the translation team from the beginning, went forward to get his Bible, he openly wept when it was handed to him, taking out his handkerchief so he could wipe away his tears.

As I sat watching this man weep, I felt prompted by the Holy Spirit with this thought: *Why don't you go tell Gaspar he is not a good return on investment?*

At that instant, I had a 180-degree turnaround in my value system. I went from thinking, "Why should we spend all this time, effort, and money for a people group of only 30,000?" to a new thought, "How are we going to make sure that all 7,000 languages on planet earth have God's Word in their heart language?"

I had no idea that one transforming moment would lead me down a path that intersected with Roy Peterson, who had recently become president at Wycliffe Bible Translators.

On June 23, 1998, a few months after my trip to Guatemala, I was in a room with leaders of a Bible movement called the International Forum of Bible Agencies. It was the first time I had attended the meeting, and it was there that I met Roy for the first time. He, along with another leader, would challenge me to start a media company, which eventually led to the release of the movie *End of the Spear.*

Neither man had ever met me, so they had no idea I had never even been inside a movie theater. Yet they felt led by God to spur me on to use media to help people see the power of God's Word to change lives.

During that meeting I also felt the Lord prompt me that someday there would be a vision so big that no ministry or financial-resource partner could fulfill it by themselves. It would be so big, in fact, that ministry partners and financial-resource partners would have to come together to reach the vision.

Fast-forward twelve years to February 2010, when I was in Guatemala with Roy, who was then the president of The Seed Company. I was there to share my story with his board of directors about what happened to me on February 7, 1998. I was thrilled to be going back to the country where God had so radically changed my life.

I was not prepared for the fact that God would again move my heart. It was on this return trip to Guatemala that the idea, a grand vision of eradicating "Bible poverty," would be birthed in me. This aligned with the vision I'd had in June 1998—and it was indeed so big that ministry partners and financial-resource partners would have to come together if we hoped to get all 7,000 languages done in our lifetime.

It was just a few months later, in May 2010, that a group of ministry partners and financial-resource partners did come together. We formed the Every Tribe Every Nation alliance, with the mission statement: "Partnering to provide God's Word in everyone's heart language in a format they can engage with, so their lives may be transformed." Roy was part of the inaugural gathering and has continued to attend the meetings, which typically are held once a month in the Admirals Club of the Dallas-Fort Worth International Airport from noon to 4:00 p.m.

Roy's experience in both business and ministry makes him a strong partner in this vision. One thing we say at Every Tribe Every Nation is, "Better Quality, Faster, and Cheaper." That describes how we want Bible translations to be done. Normally you cannot apply all three traits to a single project; you have to choose two of the three. But we believe that by coming together and partnering we can in fact create better quality Bible translations, done faster and cheaper.

The day I received the manuscript of this book to read, my Bible verse of the day was from 2 Corinthians 1:3–5, 7 (NLT):

> All praise to God, the Father of our Lord Jesus Christ. God is our merciful Father and the source of all comfort. He comforts us in all our troubles so that we can comfort others. When they are troubled, we will be able to give them the same comfort God has given us. For the more we suffer for Christ, the more God will shower us with his comfort through Christ. . . . We are confident that as you share in our sufferings, you will also share in the comfort God gives us.

After I read Roy's story, I thought, "This is a perfect verse for the book!"

Bart Gavigan, a writer for the film *End of the Spear*, once told me, "If I am going to write a movie about someone, I am going to find out what their deepest wound is, as that is where the flower grows." Both Roy and Rita are living witnesses of 2 Corinthians 1:3–5, 7;

and they exemplify Bart's belief that the "deepest wound is where the flower grows."

My prayer is that as you read this book you will be challenged to personally engage with the Scripture, with the outcome that you gain an intimate relationship with Jesus Christ. I also pray that you are stirred to become involved—to help the people of the world who are hurting, separated from hope, and those with no Bible to get the Scripture in their heart languages.

One thing that you can do right now to help is to join thousands of other believers who have committed to praying this prayer:

God, Your Word is more precious than all that I possess.
Your Scripture gives light to my path and directs my steps.
Through Your will alone lives are transformed and minds
*   made new,*
So I now pray for all people who do not yet know You.
For You've promised that Your voice by every tribe and nation
*   will be heard,*
So equip us by Your breath to provide every heart language
*   with Your Word.*

Mart Green
Chairman, Hobby Lobby

Chapter 1

AN UNCERTAIN FUTURE

You can never learn that Christ is all you
need, until Christ is all you have.

Corrie ten Boom

F ew things sound more final than a jail cell door slamming behind you. As the bars clanged shut and the Mexican guard threw home the lock, I felt fear climbing up my throat. My heart slammed against my ribs like a wild animal in a cage. The guards stared at me with hardened faces, rifles slung over their backs. They had separated me from my friends, who had been arrested with me. I was nineteen years old, terrified, helpless, and alone.

Later I would learn that because we had been in my car when we were stopped, I was considered the leader. And, since there were more than six of us involved in what we thought was going to be a one-day joyride across the Mexican border, our offenses were classified as gang activity. As far as the Mexican justice system was concerned, I was a gang leader. And I was in jail.

Getting caught by the Mexican police was the last thing on our minds on that sunny July day as we piled into my 1968 white Mercury convertible and headed out with the wind in our faces. We had debated the best route from Los Angeles to the border, but we didn't have a well-crafted plan: All we knew was that we were headed to Mexico with stolen credit cards in our pockets and fake drivers' licenses to match: unlimited spending power with plenty of time to party.

This was supposed to be the trip of a lifetime with my new LA friends. They had invited me, along with my friends Robert and Lance, to join them on this high-rolling spree. Robert and Lance had been smart enough to say no. Not me. I jumped at the chance, even offering to take my car. It felt good to be included in the excitement.

Life in the Fast Lane

I had met these new acquaintances not long after coming to California with my friends Robert and Lance. A college dropout, I had little direction in my life at the time other than "somewhere else." Arriving in Hollywood from our homes in upstate New York, the three of us thought we had landed in the middle of a dream come true when we crashed with Robert's bachelor uncle; apparently, he was willing to let us do anything we wanted. That sounded good to me; I was ready to try anything, including the array of drugs my new California friends kept on hand. Once, I watched Robert stick a needle in his vein and did nothing to stop him. I simply sat there and allowed my friend to use heroin. I never used it myself, and I have often since thought that God must have been watching over me, even then.

That morning, we all piled into my car and got on the 405 freeway, headed toward Ensenada, south of Tijuana. Before long, we had given up the debate about the best route in favor of tequila shots and beer chasers. Pretty soon, someone produced a joint, and we passed it all around, getting high and wasted as we cruised down the road at seventy miles per hour.

The guys I was with were bad characters, for sure. I remember being at a party at their house when a car backfired as it passed outside. Thinking someone was shooting at them, they reached behind pillows and under cushions and quickly produced an impressive arsenal. Apparently, they felt it was necessary to keep this kind of firepower within easy reach. This should have been a clue that I was with the wrong people.

The four-hour drive to the border flew by as we rocked down the highway with music blasting from the eight-track tape player. "Sweet Leaf," "Stairway to Heaven," and other hard-edged tunes kept us pumped up as we road-tagged our way toward Mexico. Just as we crossed into Mexico, we passed the site of a tragic head-on collision. I should have seen that as a warning.

But by the time we pulled into Ensenada, "*La Bella Cenicienta del Pacifico*"—"The Beautiful Cinderella of the Pacific"—we were more than ready for a good time, paid for by someone else's money.

When I mentioned at the beginning that we were arrested for gang activity, that might imply some sort of organized approach. But I promise you, ours was a very disorganized crime spree. We parked near the pier, piled out of the car, and headed straight for the high-end stores catering to well-heeled vacationers and *turistas*. We went into jewelry stores, leather goods shops, clothing stores . . . we hit every high-dollar place in sight. I personally selected several expensive-looking leather coats and wore one of them out of the store—on a sunny day better suited to t-shirts and cutoff jeans.

At our final stop in a jewelry store, we started to notice that it was taking the store owner a long time on the phone to get approval for our credit card purchases. At some point, the thought penetrated even our alcohol- and pot-steeped brains that our little game might be up.

We bolted from the store and ran the two blocks to my car. But before we could load up, we were surrounded by police, staring down the barrels of their weapons. Every ounce of the excitement I had felt as we started our journey earlier that day drained out of me in an instant. My pulse pounded so hard I thought I might be having a heart attack.

> "... counsel—from any number of places in Scripture—could have saved me from the heartache and abject panic that was about to overtake me."

They shoved us into the back of an old police truck with a bare metal floor and a bench seat. As I watched through the bars on the truck's enclosure, I saw them hook my car to a tow truck, headed for the impound yard. We drove a few blocks, and the truck squealed to a halt in front of the jail. Ensenada had seemed to welcome me with open, unsuspecting arms just a little while before; now I was about to see a very different side of the city.

Looking back, I realize that counsel—from any number of places in Scripture—could have saved me from the heartache and abject panic that was about to overtake me. For example, Proverbs 1:10–19, says, "My child, when sinners tempt you, don't give in. Suppose they say, 'Come on ... We'll find all kinds of riches and fill our houses with loot!' ... My child, don't go with people like that.... People like that are setting a trap for themselves. Robbery always claims the life of the robber—this is what happens to anyone who lives by violence" (GNT).

I was about to become a poster child for those who ignore the common-sense teachings of the Bible.

Doing Hard Time

Trouble had found me, as my attorney assured me when he visited me in jail, not long after my arrest. "But since this is your first offense, things should go easier for you," he said. "Your friends are bad guys. Stick with me, and I'll get you out of here."

Despite the reasonable sound of this advice, however, I would watch in disbelief when a few days later, my buddies—who obviously had a different lawyer—walked out of jail and headed home without a single backward glance. They had assured the authorities that I was, indeed, the ring leader, and that they just came along for the ride.

Meanwhile, my lawyer had me convinced that if he only had enough money, he could have me released. His words and assurances had me on an emotional roller coaster, rising to peaks of hope followed by stomach-dropping dives into despair. I told him that I had money in savings—the nest egg I had accumulated by working during high school. He persuaded the warden to let me call home and ask my folks to wire the money. He needed it for legal fees, he told me; he would get my charges dropped, and then I would be free.

The money came and went, and I never heard from my lawyer again. He had swindled me out of every dime I had; and I was still incarcerated in a Mexican jail.

For weeks afterward I cowered in a small, dirty, overcrowded room with about twenty other men, awaiting a trial date. The nights were the worst; sounds of shattering lives penetrated my ears. I never slept for longer than a few minutes at a time. One night, a man with broken bones from a car accident was tossed into the cell by the guards, who then turned and walked away without a word. To this day, his screams of pain echo in my mind. I am well above six feet tall, and the thin, filthy blanket they gave me did little to keep me warm. Most nights, I lay on the cold concrete floor and shivered as I watched the cockroaches scuttle across the cell.

Our "toilet" was a hole in the floor; our "faucet" was a small pipe that dripped water. The place reeked of urine, feces, and body odor. The food was miserable and doled out in small portions. Poor nutrition and abdominal bacteria combined to cause rapid weight loss, accompanied by wracking pain in my gut.

But worse than all this was my inability to communicate with someone—anyone—in my native language. Once my attorney had vanished, I had no idea, even a false idea, of what was happening outside the cell or with my legal case. Never in my life have I been more alone, more isolated, or more afraid.

One day, the guards unlocked the door, pointed at me, and shuffled me into a courtroom that looked like something from a 1930s movie. The floor was made of rough-hewn wooden planks, and it creaked with every limping step I took toward the judge who now held my destiny in his hands.

I stood alone in that courtroom, far from home; no one stood beside me, and no one was there with me to plead my case. I was allowed to make no phone calls, and the only person who had given me any advice was long gone, along with all my money.

When the judge, in Spanish, asked me how I pled to the charges against me, I said the only word I knew: "*Culpado*"—"guilty." He sentenced me to almost five years in prison, with more charges pending.

A Glimmer of Hope

Walking out of the courtroom that day, I was facing nearly five years in prison, with the possibility of another four years if federal charges were filed against me. At nineteen years of age, I was transferred to a larger prison that held an even more dangerous population. I was living in a place beyond fear: stark terror was my almost constant companion. I knew

> "I was living in a place beyond fear: stark terror was my almost constant companion."

I could never survive for five years in such a place. My life was over.

One day, an inmate approached me. I braced myself for the worst, and then he spoke to me in English. He said his name was Raul, and he soon told me that he had been a hit man for the Mexican equivalent of the Mafia. He was in here for murder.

I sat and listened as Raul described the secret compartment he had built into the dashboard of his car. With the push of a button, he told me, the compartment popped open to give access to his weapon of choice. Even though I was nervous, realizing that I was talking to an actual assassin, I realized I was also intrigued.

The "what-are-you-in-for" talk turned in my direction, and I explained my situation to Raul. By this time, an Anglo guy named

Paul, from Newport Beach, had joined us. Paul told me that he had been making regular drug runs into Mexico in his luxury Chrysler fitted with fake panels. Shuttling marijuana from Mexico to his clients in California had been very lucrative for Paul until he was busted. By this time, he was about two years into a five-year sentence, he said.

Paul appeared to be about the age of my dad, which made it easier for me to look up to him and trust him. I shared with him my wild, yet very real, plans to escape. Being in that jail felt never-ending, and I was desperate to get out. Not seeing any hope in sight, I put together very detailed plans to escape. I was young, naïve, scared, and hopeless.

Paul sat patiently, listening to this young kid fantasize about something he knew could never be realistic. When I finished, he said, "I had some of the same ideas, but after I worked through all the details, none of them made sense."

And then, with Paul looking on, Raul said to me, "God can get you through this, Roy. Jesus Christ has changed my life, and He can change yours, too."

If there was anything these guys could have said to me in that moment that would have been more unexpected, I don't know what it would have been. I stared, open-mouthed, from Raul to Paul, and they looked back at me with faces that gave every evidence of being serious. *Nothing makes any sense*, I thought.

They both had Spanish Bibles with them. They invited me to come to their Bible study. They were pretty much the first people who had spoken to me in English since I'd been arrested. It's hard for me to describe the emotions I felt at being invited and included. So, I went. It was just the three of us.

As I began to spend time with Paul and Raul, I started to notice that both of these guys, despite being convicted criminals, had an atmosphere of peace about them that was completely at odds with our desperate surroundings. They translated every verse they read from their Bibles into English, beginning with the Gospel According to Matthew. We worked through the genealogical lists, trying to figure out what that had to do with our lives.

Though I had not thought about God in a long time, I slowly began to wish for the kind of peace that Raul and Paul appeared to have. They talked to me about it, telling me that if I confessed my sins to God and accepted His grace, I could be forgiven and have a fresh start. I didn't understand how something like that could overturn all the bad things I had done and all that had happened to me, but I kept listening. I wasn't ready to do anything as radical as turn my life over to God, but I also wasn't walking away. It astounds me, looking back, that I was so stubborn and prideful. After all, it wasn't as though I was doing all that well on my own.

> "Though I had not thought about God in a long time, I slowly began to wish for the kind of peace that Raul and Paul appeared to have."

Prisons within Prisons

Sitting alone in that prison cell in Mexico, I felt powerless, isolated, and afraid. Of course, I was almost completely focused, especially at first, on my bodily imprisonment and its likely consequences for my physical well-being and future.

But sadly, I was almost completely unaware of my spiritual imprisonment. I now realize that my spiritual blindness and poverty was the real reason I was in prison in Mexico. A lack of biblical principles to guide me had led me to a series of lousy decisions that had culminated in my arrest and imprisonment.

My life apart from God and His Word had put me in a prison of my own making—a prison of the spirit. I would eventually learn that the only path to true freedom is the one promised by Christ, when He said, "If the Son sets you free, then you will be really free" (John 8:36, GNT). I fervently hope that you never experience the type of terror that swallowed me when I crouched in a stinking prison cell full of desperate, dangerous men. I have actually learned to be thankful for that awful experience, because it taught me something I would probably not have learned any other way: When your soul is imprisoned by sin, the only path to freedom is through the Word of God in the Bible.

> "A lack of biblical principles to guide me had led me to a series of lousy decisions that had culminated in my arrest and imprisonment."

When I took that ill-fated jaunt to Ensenada, I thought I had a purpose, but really, the only thing on my mind was having a good time. I had no concept of possible consequences for my actions, and certainly no sense of responsibility for the bad decisions I had made. What I needed in my life—as I soon came to realize—was the purpose and commitment provided by my Creator and Father. I needed to know why I was on this planet and what I needed to be doing while I was here: all questions that have their ultimate answers in God's Word.

In other words, what I needed, even though I didn't know it, was transformation. Only by opening my life to the Word of God would I ever be able to experience the freedom that Jesus promises.

I will be forever grateful to God that He brought Raul and Paul into my life that day, in a dirty cell in Mexico. Even though all we had to work with was the Bible in Spanish, these two unlikely "preachers" were able to introduce God's Word to someone who desperately needed it. Once I began to gain a "God's-eye view" of life, I slowly became empowered to move beyond fear, uncertainty, and purposelessness into a life filled with hope, direction, and promise—even in a prison cell.

By the grace of God, I was soon to have just such an

> **"I needed to know why I was on this planet and what I needed to be doing while I was here: all questions that have their ultimate answers in God's Word."**

encounter with His living and active Word. Because of that encounter, my life was changed, and I was set free, even though, for a time, my body was still locked away down in Mexico. I was about to make the most important discovery of my life: I was about to discover the key to real freedom—a key that no one could ever take away.

Food for Thought

- Not all prisons have bars and locks; some exist only in the hearts and minds of people.

- The only path to true freedom is the one promised by Christ, when He said, "If the Son sets you free, then you will be really free" (John 8:36, GNT).

- We can introduce people to the transforming Word of God and the freedom it brings.

Questions to Consider

1. What would it be like not being able to communicate with anyone in your native language? What limitations do you encounter in expressing thoughts, feelings, or needs?

2. When in your life have you felt most powerless or vulnerable? What brought on these feelings? Where did you turn for help?

3. Did someone introduce you to God's Word? Have you introduced someone else to God's Word? What were those experiences like?

Chapter 2

THE BOOK THAT CHANGED EVERYTHING

---

*When you read God's Word, you must constantly be
saying to yourself, "It is talking to me, and about me."*

Søren Kierkegaard

One day some "Jesus freaks" (as we called them at the time)
from Southern California showed up at the prison. These
long-haired hippies in flip-flops and bell-bottomed jeans were a
brand-new kind of interesting for many of the men in the prison.
Of course, in prison, when day after day drags along in the same
fashion, anything different becomes an oasis in the desert of same-
ness. There was a flurry of activity as the guards and other prison
administrators set up the meeting.

Before long, prisoners were filing into the assembly room to
jockey for seats so they could see the show. I was there, too; not only
did I have some interest in what they might say, given my ongoing
conversations with Raul and Paul, but like the rest of the inmates,
I was eager for anything to break up the usual routine.

The whole meeting, of course, was in Spanish, even the songs.
But for some reason, that day, it didn't matter. When the long-haired

evangelists broke out their guitars and sang Scripture-filled songs, it seemed to me as though the universal language of love filled the room. The Holy Spirit rushed in. Peace washed over me: a feeling that I hadn't experienced since that fateful day when I was arrested with my friends.

Something about these folks simply oozed the love of Jesus and His compassion. After the meeting, Paul, Raul, and I talked to them.

"Dude, what's your story?" one of them asked me.

> **"I had a burning desire in my heart to read God's Word in my own language, and knowing that this could soon be possible just made the wait seem that much longer."**

They listened quietly as I told them all the details. They empathized with me about what the crooked attorney had done. It felt good to tell my side of things. They communicated to me that they genuinely understood why I feared for my life each day. They truly cared. They prayed for me and encouraged me.

"Do you have an English Bible you could give me?" I asked.

"Man, you're doing time in Mexico and can't speak Spanish?" They couldn't believe it. All they had with them were Spanish Bibles, but they promised to bring me an English version when they returned in a month.

Let me tell you, that month seemed longer than any month I had ever lived through. I had a burning desire in my heart to read God's Word in my own language, and knowing that this could soon be possible just made the wait seem that much longer.

True to their word, when they came back, not only did they bring me a Bible, but they also brought English Bibles for Paul and Raul. Raul no longer had to translate for me, verse by verse. When I got that English Bible in my hands, it felt as if I was holding a piece of freedom. In a way, I guess, that's exactly what it was.

Words of Life

I cherished my new gift. Something strange and wonderful happened to me. Perhaps it was because I had just received something of great value in the midst of a deadly situation. Perhaps I cherished that Bible because I had to wait a month to get a copy of Scripture I could read for myself. Or maybe I just sensed it held the key to my freedom. But for whatever reason, on that bright day when they put that Bible in my hands, my life took a sharp upward turn.

I consumed God's Word like the dying man I was. Later, I would read some words from Jeremiah that described exactly how I felt: "You spoke to me, and I listened to every word. I belong to you, Lord God Almighty, and so your words filled my heart with joy and happiness" (Jeremiah 15:16, GNT). It was exactly like that for me; I had been starving to death, spiritually, and now I had a never-ending feast at my fingertips.

One night on that prison floor, it wasn't the tattered blanket I clutched, but my Bible instead. I confessed my sins and failures. "I need You, Lord! I need Your help," I cried out to God. "If You're willing to take my life, it's Yours. Without You, my life is over."

That night, I grabbed hold of His all-powerful forgiveness with both fists and held on tight. At that moment, I escaped! To paraphrase the words of Paul to the Colossian Christians, the Lord rescued me from the kingdom of darkness and transferred me into "the kingdom of his dear Son" (Colossians 1:13). As I cried out to God from the depths of my soul, I felt a crushing weight lifted from my heart.

When I got up off the floor, I couldn't wait for morning to come so I could tell Raul and Paul what had happened to me. "It's about time!" Paul said. They pounded me on the back and grinned. Then we dove into our new Bibles. In the following weeks and months, if we weren't eating or sleeping, Paul, Raul, and I were consuming God's Word together.

> "... I grabbed hold of His all-powerful forgiveness with both fists and held on tight."

From that day on, nothing mattered more to me than God and His Word. Not the stench, not the bugs, not the rashes, not the threats, not the fear. Later, when I found Psalm 91 in my Bible, it became a lifeline: "His faithfulness will protect and defend you. You need not fear any dangers at night or sudden attacks during the day or the plagues that strike in the dark or the evils that kill in the daylight. A thousand may fall dead beside you, ten thousand all around you, but you will not be harmed" (Psalm 91:4–7, GNT).

God's providence was at work in my life. I sensed He had a purpose for me, although I couldn't begin to dream how this experience at nineteen years of age would define the rest of my life.

One day it came to me that, though nothing had changed for me on the outside, everything had changed on the inside. No longer did I dread facing each day. Why should I? God greeted me every morning. I was still desperate to get out of prison, but now it was different. His Holy Spirit met me the moment I cracked open His Word. Day by day, He led me deeper into Scripture and taught me His promises and precepts. It was a treasure that no one—no guard, no dangerous inmate, no crooked lawyer—nobody—could take away from me.

> "One day it came to me that, though nothing had changed for me on the outside, everything had changed on the inside."

For the first time since I had been thrown into a cell months before, I knew, with a certainty that I could not explain, that I would live and not die in that place. I knew that I had done wrong and that I deserved the punishment the Mexican court had handed down. "I'm ready to serve my sentence," I told the Lord. "Except for a miracle, I know I'll be here for the entire time."

Except for a miracle . . .

When God Spoke My Language

No matter how grateful I will always be for Raul and Paul, who began sharing the Scriptures with me in Spanish—and slowly, painstakingly translating it into English for me—everything changed when I was finally able to read the Bible in my own language. It was as if I could hear God's voice in my heart as I read His Word: teaching me, comforting me, and giving me hope. I think that in many ways, the experience of encountering the Bible in my own tongue, deep in the bowels of that Mexican prison, is what would later convince me of the absolutely vital need to make the Bible available to every person on earth in his or her own language. After all, if God's Word could transform a hired killer, a drug smuggler, and a rebellious, unmotivated nineteen-year-old, it could transform anybody!

Through the years, I have reflected on the power of God's Word that night on the floor of my prison cell. I have concluded—and my subsequent experience has confirmed—that there is nothing more powerful than the Word of God, read and understood in a person's heart language—for me, English—encountered at a time when a person's life

> "... there is nothing more powerful than the Word of God, read and understood in a person's heart language"

has been made ready to receive it. My imprisonment made me wide open; I knew I needed a rescuer, a Savior! And when I was able to read the Bible in English, I realized that I had found what I needed . . . and that my Savior had found me.

Not only did God come into my heart and save me that night, He also gave me a purpose and a direction in life. He planted a seed deep in my soul that has grown into a burning desire to help other people who are also in desperate need of a Savior, just as I was. I know what it means to feel lost, alone, and directionless. But once I was able to get my hands on the Word of God and read it for myself, I knew I would never be alone again. In the same way, it has been both the burden and the joy of my life to make that same experience possible for other people all around the world.

Imagine with me that someone took your English Bible away and replaced it with a version in a different language. Then you had no alternative, forever, but to read the Bible and attend a church that was not in your language.

This is something like the situation I was in, except that my only exposure to the Spanish language was the little bit I could snag from the conversations happening around me. Every day I was faced with an onslaught of words I didn't know, expressions I didn't recognize, warnings I couldn't understand. Already under almost unbearable stress from trying to survive each day in a hostile, uncaring environment, I faced the additional stress of trying desperately to skim enough information from context, facial expressions, and gestures to allow me to function in an environment dominated by what was, to me, an unintelligible language. Taken together, it was completely overwhelming.

Even when Raul, Paul, and I were doing our Bible study, the language barrier was still there. Though both of them did their best to help the Spanish words in their Bibles make sense to my American English ears, it was slow and laborious. There are certain nuances that you don't understand unless you are reading or listening in your native language. And there is a huge difference between having an intellectual understanding of the general meaning and having the words speak directly to your soul. That direct connection that I so longed for was what was missing—and the joy of finding it flooded my heart when I was finally able to hold an English-language Bible in my hands.

As I learned in a Mexican prison cell, God's Word in the Bible contains the advice, instruction, and wisdom that every person most needs in order to live life to its fullest—and also to have hope for life everlasting. But when those words don't exist in the heart language of a people, it is excruciatingly difficult for them to gain the maximum benefit from this life-giving source.

> "... God's Word
> in the Bible contains
> the advice, instruction,
> and wisdom that every
> person most needs in
> order to live life to its
> fullest—and also to have
> hope for life everlasting."

It is almost impossible for me to adequately describe for those who have not personally witnessed such events the astounding power that is unleashed when people read the Scriptures in their own language for the first time. Suffice it to say that phrases like "God keeps every promise he makes" (Proverbs 30:5, GNT); "The word of our God endures forever" (Isaiah 40:8, GNT); "The Word of God is alive and active" (Hebrews 4:12, GNT); and "the living and eternal word of God" (1 Peter 1:23, GNT) take on a whole new meaning when the Bible is made available to those who have not previously had the opportunity for a personal experience with God's transforming Word.

A Different Type of Poverty

Most reading these words live, as I do, in the relative ease and security of modern western society. By the mercy and grace of God, not many of us need to worry about going to bed with an empty stomach. Most of us are blessed with the knowledge that we will sleep tonight in a safe place, probably behind locked doors. Very few, if any, of us are actively worried about facing life-threatening danger during the course of a typical day, and I doubt if many of us must deal with the complete unavailability of medical resources in the face of a disease, either our own or one affecting our children or other loved ones.

And yet, when I was in that Mexican prison, I lived each day with these types of deprivation. I didn't have enough to eat, and often the food that was available made me sick. I was surrounded by danger almost all the time; when I lay down at night, I never felt assurance that I would wake the next morning. During the period of my incarceration, I lived with many of the same circumstances as people in some of the world's most difficult and dangerous places—except

> "... as tragic and harmful as physical poverty is, there is a type of poverty rampant in our world that has even worse, more long-lasting consequences. I am talking about biblical poverty."

that they have lived that way for generations in some cases. That experience has created in me an empathy for those who endure physical poverty and deprivation.

Nevertheless, as tragic and harmful as physical poverty is, there is a type of poverty rampant in our world that has even worse, more long-lasting consequences. I am talking about biblical poverty.

Biblical poverty is the condition of people for whom the Bible is unavailable. This is the situation I was in before Raul and Paul invited me into their tiny fellowship, before those "missionaries in sandals" brought me my English Bible. Not only did I have to deal with the day-to-day struggle for existence forced upon me by the deprivation of prison life, but I also had to do so in a state of biblical poverty that robbed me of hope, faith, and the emotional resilience that can be provided by God's Word alone. At the very time when I was most in need of the strength the Bible can provide, I was also the most bereft of this never-ending source of power and confidence. Today, in many parts of the world, people are, through no fault of their own, in the same situation that I was in while doing hard time in Mexico.

> "... we absolutely must do everything in our power to alleviate hunger, disease, illiteracy, and all the other debilitating effects that physical poverty wreaks on human lives. But at the same time, we must be just as determined to conquer biblical poverty. Only by addressing both of these voids in human lives can we ever hope to offer true and lasting healing to a world in desperate need."

Please don't mistake me; we absolutely must do everything in our power to alleviate hunger, disease, illiteracy, and all the other debilitating effects that physical poverty wreaks on human lives. But at the same time, we must be just as determined to conquer biblical poverty. Only by addressing both of these voids in human lives can we ever hope to offer true and lasting healing to a world in desperate need.

I know several people who are active with local animal rescue organizations. For these folks, the sight of an abandoned dog or cat, alone and scared on the street as it tries to fend for itself, is an unbearable tragedy. They are compelled to give the animal a safe place to live and food to eat while seeking a permanent home for it. In fact, I know several such individuals who have acquired a number of household pets in this very way! They would rather make space for "one more" than allow that dog or cat to face a hostile, uncaring environment on its own. I'm grateful to know people who are actively committed to the welfare of helpless strays; their caring hearts make our communities better places to live.

But how I long for more of those who might be willing to become activists for the biblically impoverished! As I reflect on my own life, I know that without one of those rag-tagged ambassadors of the Gospel caring enough about me to find and bring to my prison cell an English translation of the Bible, I might never have known the surpassing peace of God's presence in my heart. And without the committed and active concern of workers and supporters of the world Bible movement, thousands of human souls may never hear the words of life spoken in their own language. That is a tragedy that our hurting world simply cannot afford.

Food for Thought

- Genuine engagement with the Bible transforms lives.

- Now more than ever, we must become partners with God in taking His Word to everyone, in every language, using every means at our disposal.

- Only by addressing physical, emotional, and spiritual poverty can we offer true and lasting healing to a world in desperate need.

Questions to Consider

1. Have you ever tried to communicate with someone or read something in a language that you knew only a little? What was it like?

2. How would your life be different without access to the Bible?

3. What types of poverty have you experienced in your life— physical, spiritual, emotional? What is it like to lack the resources you need to thrive?

Chapter 3

THE KINDNESS OF A STRANGER

---

*He was still a long way from home when his father
saw him; his heart was filled with pity, and he ran,
threw his arms around his son, and kissed him.*

Luke 15:20, GNT

I don't know if you have ever had a child or other loved one who was in desperate circumstances; I pray that this will never happen to you. But while I was in prison in Mexico, my father, back home in upstate New York, was in agony. His son, whom he loved, was in one of the most perilous of places, and he felt powerless to do anything to help.

Nevertheless, Dad never stopped trying to figure out a way to come to my aid. With the tenacious love of a father, he refused to believe there wasn't something he could do to get his son out of prison.

The Love of a Father

William Peterson, also known as Bill Senior, was a leader and powerful man, standing six feet tall and weighing 300 pounds. He provided for our family as a wholesale beer salesman. Dad also was an accomplished musician, an attribute that I loved about him. The jazz band he formed was frequently in demand all around our area at home. He loved the stage. He was a leader. Needless to say, if my dad was in a room, people knew it.

He was also accustomed to getting things done, so not long after my arrest, taking his usual direct approach, he and my brother, Bill Junior, hopped on a plane to San Diego. After they landed, Dad and Bill rented a car and drove down the coast to Ensenada. Their first stop was the US Consulate's office. Dad wanted to look the people directly in the eye and resolve the situation, right then and there.

He couldn't; the US consulate told him that under the circumstances, there was nothing they could do. Dad and my brother left that meeting dejected and drove to the prison with no hope of helping me. Shadows of sadness hung down their faces as they stood at the reinforced steel doors, waiting to see me. When they were cleared to enter, my stern, no-nonsense father instantly wrapped me in his powerful arms. Tears rolled down his face as he choked out the words, "There is nothing I can do to get you released."

It was the first time in my life I ever saw my dad cry. He was a broken father, holding a broken son.

Dad and Bill saw some of the sordid details of my everyday life. As Dad and I paced the courtyard, the stench was overwhelming. At one end of the yard, only a flimsy wall stood between the communal showers and the five-seat row of cement bench toilets. Dad and I were embarrassed as we walked past threadbare blankets hung up to partition space for conjugal visits. We watched young children who should have been playing on a playground, but instead were running around the dirty prison yard while visiting their fathers or older brothers. I could see in my father's eyes, as he looked around, the pain of the realization that this was what his son had come to. When he saw the area I shared with thirty to forty other men, he lowered his head, fighting the tears that gently fell.

I told Dad that there were some bright spots in my life, too; it wasn't all bad. I introduced him to a few people like Juan, who was so kind to me. Just a humble farmer, Juan had grown marijuana for a living . . . until he got caught with three tons of it on his farm.

Of course, Dad met Paul and Raul. I told him how they had included me and that we read the Bible together. I was too unsure of myself spiritually to say much to Dad about my encounter with the Lord. I didn't think I could explain the Gospel so that he and Bill would understand.

As Dad prepared to leave that last day, he shoved a small sum of money into my hand. That meant I could buy a few things from the *tienda*, which was run by long-term inmates who had purchased— or bribed to obtain—the right to open the little store. I was eager to have eggs. A small bowl of cereal in the morning and a bowl of soup for lunch and some rice and black beans for dinner every day just didn't cut it. (At that moment, a few eggs cooked over a borrowed propane burner tasted better to me than about anything I had ever eaten!)

Dad then stood up from the cement bench where we had been seated. He hugged my thin frame. His baritone voice cracked as he said, "I will get your car out of the impoundment yard. Bill and I will drive it back to New York. It'll be there when you come home."

When he said the word "home," I almost couldn't bear it. The thought of the comfortable place I had lived—the place I had been so eager, and foolish enough, to leave—seemed like a golden dream, right then. Entirely unattainable.

Then Dad and Bill walked the cobbled streets to their hotel for their last night in town before the long drive home. They went to the hotel restaurant and sat at a table. The owner walked over, looked at Dad, and said in broken English, "Señor Peterson, something is wrong. What is going on?"

My father, a man who never talked about personal problems with family members, much less strangers, shared the whole story. "My son did some bad things," Dad said. "And an attorney stole all his money and never represented him."

"I'll find out who he is. I'll have his legs broken," the owner offered. "Just give me $300 and I'll take care of it."

"That will not help my son."

The owner immediately felt the pain of a brokenhearted father. He looked around and then said, "The man at the table next to you is someone who should hear what has happened to your son." That man was a judge.

Even though Dad was embarrassed to go over the details again, he told the judge what I had done and what had happened to me. The judge assured my father he would make it right.

"On December 10, I will be seated in my court and I will issue a release for your son," the judge said. "Purchase bus tickets out of the country and airline tickets for your son now. Give them to this hotel owner. Tell your son to come to this hotel immediately after his release. He can pick up the tickets and then make his way back home."

In spite of the ordeal I'd been through and everything else that had happened, including the false promises of the attorney, my dad believed this judge. The next day he purchased bus tickets to the border and airline tickets from San Diego to New York for the date the judge told him. Dad gave the tickets to the hotel owner. Then he and my brother drove out of town.

The judge came to see me in prison after they left. He laid out the details for me exactly as he had explained them to my father.

But his words reminded me of my attorney's lies, and doubts flooded my mind. I was afraid to believe that my freedom could really be at hand, that anything they told me could be trusted. My friends Raul and Paul, who had also seen more than their share of the inner workings of the justice system, further fueled my doubt. But together we hoped against hope as we waited out the weeks and counted the days. Could it really be possible that God was about to deliver what seemed to me like an absolute miracle? I hoped and prayed, day after day and night after night, that it was so.

The month of December arrived, and soon after that, some guards came to stand in front of the prison door. "Peterson, Roy!" one of them shouted in his thick Spanish accent.

I stood up and walked toward him, hardly daring to breathe. One of the other guards brought out a key. The door to my cell was opened. My heart raced as I stepped through.

I followed a guard to the next door. It opened. Then another door opened to an office. In that office there was an open door to the street. Yes, the door was wide open, and I could see the city street and sidewalk and sunshine! My heart raced even more with anticipation. Someone thumped down a stack of papers written in Spanish and handed me a pen, gesturing for me to sign. I did so without hesitation, even though I couldn't read one word of what I was signing. As far as I could discern from what was being said,

I was released on some kind of parole. I might have to report in every month. This little-understood detail would haunt me for years.

When You Can't Do It Yourself

Our American culture deeply values individual initiative and the "can-do" spirit. We pride ourselves on our ability to take care of ourselves, to pull ourselves up by our own bootstraps. We are fond of saying that in our country people can accomplish anything they set their minds to, as long as they are determined and willing to work both hard and smart. Much of our admiration of such qualities stems, of course, from our frontier heritage: our heroes are those who faced impossible odds and overcame harsh obstacles in order to create a better life or to take advantage of a great opportunity. This is a worthy heritage, and we can celebrate it.

> "There are times in each person's life when, like it or not, we cannot make it on our own power. At some time or other, each one of us is going to need help."

But no matter how much I tried, I was unable to rescue myself from that Mexican prison. No matter how hard I might have pulled on my bootstraps—if I had even had any bootstraps—I wasn't going anywhere! Even my big, strong father, who always knew how to get things done, couldn't make it happen. We required the help of a kind stranger—a kind hotel owner and a judge who had compassion on my father and me.

There are times in each person's life when, like it or not, we cannot make it on our own power. At some time or other, each one of us is going to need help. Like Jonah, when he was thrashing about in the stormy ocean, all of us, at some time or other, will experience the terror of helplessness: "The water came over me and choked me; the sea covered me completely, and seaweed wrapped around my head" (Jonah 2:5, GNT).

At times like these, no matter how great our determination or our will to succeed, and no matter how much we are willing to help ourselves, we cannot make it alone. We need a rescuer. We need someone who, in the words of the Psalmist, can lift us "out of a dangerous pit, out of the deadly quicksand"; someone who can set our feet on a rock and give us a firm place to stand (Psalm 40:2, GNT). In other words, we need God.

> ". . . God is our only hope; His presence, often mediated through His people, is the only thing that can save."

This is especially true when we are in the pit of spiritual despair: when the slimy mud of our own bad choices or difficult circumstances traps us and prevents us from climbing into the light. In these times, God is our only hope; His presence, often mediated through His people, is the only thing that can save.

Transformation of a Troublemaker

This was certainly the case for my friend Naphtaly Mattah. He could hardly have been placed in a more helpless situation. Born into a family of ten children amid crushing poverty on Mfangano Island in Kenya's Lake Victoria, Naphtaly should, by all rights, have died in infancy, as six of his siblings did, each before the age of five years. He relates that as a child, he was once in a coma for three days and was not expected to survive. But God reached down into Naphtaly's spirit and preserved his life, because, as Naphtaly is convinced, God had a plan for him.

Determined to escape the impoverished existence into which he was born, Naphtaly studied hard in school. There was no electricity in his home—not even a kerosene lantern. So Naphtaly sat close to the fire in the evenings as he did his lessons. Not surprisingly, he was first in his class in school.

When he was older, he had to leave home and live with a cousin in the town of Lamu, where he received medical treatment for a spinal problem. The cousin's wife treated him like an indentured servant, including beatings and frequent predictions that he would never amount to anything. But while he was there, he discovered a pamphlet written in the Swahili he had learned in school; it was the Gospel of Matthew. "The words of Jesus captivated me," he said. "That planted a seed and a quest in my heart."

Winning an academic scholarship to attend university, Naphtaly jumped at the chance. But then, he acquired some friends who did not have strong values. He began to drink excessively and to live the party life. Not only that, but he got involved in some organizations that, though nominally working for students' rights, often resorted to violent tactics. He was a born leader, and before long, he was one of those who instigated riots and engaged in other dangerous behaviors.

The turning point in Naphtaly Mattah's life came when one of his newfound friends literally drank himself to death. Naphtaly and some of his friends attended the funeral and afterward stopped at a local eatery, where their behavior become obnoxious and rowdy.

An elderly woman sat in the back, observing their ruckus. While other patrons left the establishment, made uneasy by Naphtaly and his gang, she stayed. Unafraid, she beckoned to Naphtaly, "My son, please come here."

Because of the respect for elders that is ingrained in his culture, Naphtaly went over to the old woman.

"Son, sit down," she said. "Do you know that Jesus Christ died for you and He wants you to be His servant right now?"

"Mam," he said, using a term of deference for this elderly woman, "look at me. Do you think the way I am I can become a Christian?"

The wizened old woman steadily held Naphtaly's gaze. "My son, don't despise yourself. The Jesus I am telling you about knows you the way you are," she said. "On your own, you cannot make yourself good and then come to Him. But if you say 'yes,' He will come into your life right now."

No doubt, something clicked for Naphtaly; the words he had read in the Gospel of Matthew, all those years ago, flooded back into his mind. "There was a struggle inside," Naphtaly recalled. "But I said 'yes.' And a great weight was removed."

Later Naphtaly looked for "Mam," but he couldn't find her. He asked around at churches and other local places, but no one seemed to know this little elderly woman who had drastically changed his life. Was she an angel sent by God? Naphtaly wonders to this day.

Naphtaly Mattah became involved in a local church. In the months that followed, he read the English Bible from cover to cover, often weeping as he thought about the darkness and hopelessness of his Suba people on the island where they lived. In 1990, Naphtaly went home to Mfangano Island to preach to his people and to build churches, with the help of some university students he had recruited. Not long after, when he returned to the island, he found that the churches they had built were torn down and that the people were scattered. Naphtaly said that God revealed to him that the Suba people needed a Bible in their own language. He moved back to the island permanently, started another church, and began translating the Bible into Suba.

Today, Naphtaly and his wife, Nereah, minister to homeless children, many of them orphaned by the African HIV/AIDS epidemic that began in the 1990s. They run Gethsemane Garden Christian Centre, providing housing and education services for children aged three through nine. Mfangano Island has become, instead of a place of despair and poverty, a beacon of hope and healing to hundreds of children.

But none of this would have been possible if Naphtaly had insisted on "rescuing" himself by his own efforts, using his own judgment. As "Mam" told him, it was impossible for him to make himself acceptable to God; he had to receive God's favor as a free gift, just as I received the kindness of the Mexican judge. Naphtaly could not save himself; for that, he needed God.

Since placing his trust in God, Naphtaly Mattah has been an agent for transformation among the Suba people. By making it possible for them to read God's Word in their own language, Naphtaly has put into their hands the single greatest source of power in the universe. Now, instead of leading riots in order to effect change, he leads people to God.

Food for Thought

- There are times in all of our lives when we can't rescue ourselves.

- In these times, God is our only hope; His presence, often mediated through others, is the only thing that can save us.

- When we receive God's favor as a free gift, we are transformed and can be used to transform others.

Questions to Consider

1. When have you needed help, unable to do something on your own? Was it difficult to ask for help? What barriers did you have to overcome?

2. Think of a person who has done something for you that you can never repay. How do you feel about that person? Has this gift given you a different perspective on helping others?

3. Has reading the Bible given you a burden for a specific group of people or need in the world? What practical step could the Bible's words be prompting you to take?

Chapter 4

THE SMELL OF FREEDOM

I've been lost in a fantasy that blinded me /
Until your love broke through.

Keith Green

I had just finished signing the papers the prison official put in front of me, and I was afraid to breathe, afraid even to admit to myself that my dream of freedom might be about to come true. What if it was just another trick to get money? What if I had just signed something in Spanish that I didn't understand and they used it to put me away for even longer?

More papers were shoved my way; I signed them. Then a guard motioned toward the door, and through it I saw the outside world. My heart felt more excitement than I'd ever experienced in my life as the guard gestured again toward the street.

I stepped into bright sunlight, free that morning for the first time in nearly five months. I breathed in fresh air—free air!—and looked at the blue sky as I thanked God. The normal, everyday street scenes taking place around me seemed miraculous: shop owners outside low, whitewashed adobe storefronts sweeping their walkways using worn-down brooms and buckets of water; women with baskets over their arms, walking along the side of the street; skinny dogs sleeping in the sun—it was as if I were seeing normal life for the first time. Everything looked so beautiful and full of color.

Both exhilaration and fear flooded my emotions. I couldn't really breathe easily until I was back in the US. With the instructions from the incredibly generous judge clutched tightly in my hand, I wound my way through Ensenada. Although I'd been there for five months I did not know the city or the streets. *Turn right at this crossroad. Go two blocks. Turn left at the fountain. Lord, please help me get home!*

I found the hotel, where the very kind owner greeted me with a warm smile and a firm handshake. I sensed that he felt he was righting a wrong in his city. He guided me to the bus stop. I wanted more than anything to waste no time in putting as much distance as possible between that prison and me.

At the bus station, I paced nervously until it was finally time to board. I stepped onto that overcrowded bus, filled with the sounds of babies crying, women and men talking. It was a beautiful cacophony: the sound of freedom with the promise of home. It was also the sound of God's plan clicking into place for the next leg of my life's journey.

The ride from Ensenada to San Diego lasted a couple of hours, but the time passed for me in a swirl of gratitude and relief, though with a background aroma of anxiety. But when our bus finally drove onto American soil, I stopped holding my breath. *I'm safe. They can't change their minds now. I'm really going home.*

When I got off the bus at the San Diego airport and boarded a plane for New York, I sat down, closed my eyes, and thought about facing my family, my friends, and the choices I'd made to land in a Mexican prison. For years I would struggle with deep shame. I had hours in front of me to reflect on the past five months. Above all, I marveled at God's love and mercy to rescue me. I was free.

But as I stepped from the plane onto the tarmac at the small Albany International Airport, the shame nearly paralyzed me. I was coming back into the arms of a family who loved me: a family I had walked away from seven months before because of my immaturity, selfishness, and foolish desires.

Admittedly, there had not been a big spiritual aspect of my life as a young boy. My parents believed in God, and my mom often said a simple prayer over me when she put me to bed at night—something within the "now I lay me down to sleep" variety. There was even a picture of Jesus hanging in my bedroom, maybe from my mother's childhood.

> "... the shame nearly paralyzed me. I was coming back into the arms of a family who loved me: a family I had walked away from seven months before because of my immaturity, selfishness, and foolish desires."

But my main memories of anything church-related are connected to my older sister, Karen. When she was a young teenager, she became interested in the Christian faith and started dragging her younger siblings—my sister Janice and me—to church, Sunday school, Vacation Bible School, and any other gathering she could find out about. But she was nine years older, and before I knew it she left for college. All of that pretty much ended once she left.

When I was fifteen, the only thing my friends and I could talk about was the Woodstock Festival, taking place not far from our home. All the musicians I loved—The Who, Creedence Clearwater Revival, Hendrix, Joplin, Dylan, Joe Cocker—were going to be there, and I wanted desperately to attend. Tickets were only $18 in advance, I told my parents.

"You're not going!" The message from my mom and dad was unequivocal, loud, and clear. There would be no discussion and no appeal. Somehow they knew.

The Making of a Prodigal

I was filled with righteous, teenaged indignation. How could my folks be so uncool? Didn't they understand how important this music was, this event? Rock 'n' roll history was about to be made, and they were denying me my part in it! And I didn't even know how historic it would be.

This was the time in my young life when I began to harbor feelings of rebellion and a desire for independence at any cost. All that unfocused longing and shortsighted, youthful impatience would culminate, a couple of years later, in my travel to southern California and the subsequent venture that would land me in a Mexican prison. I was practically reenacting the story of the Prodigal Son; but instead of munching on seed pods in a pig pen, I had been slurping thin soup in a prison cell.

Now, that prodigal walked the tarmac at the Albany airport. It seemed like a lifetime had passed since I had been home. I struggled to grasp the reality of Romans 8:1 as I marched toward the terminal to face my family. "There is no condemnation now for those who live in union with Christ Jesus" (GNT).

Why should they care about me after I'd spent the last five months incarcerated for a crime I had committed? I'd failed Dad. I'd caused Mom, Karen, and Janice sleepless nights. Surely my brother must resent me, I thought. I didn't know what it had cost my parents financially, and they would never tell me. As God gives us His grace, they had freely given me this gift of freedom and acceptance.

I walked into the terminal on that December day and they drew me into warm hugs as I shivered from the bone-chilling cold outside. Mom and Janice cried tears of joy. Dad hugged me as if I had just won the Heisman trophy. Then, they placed a heavy winter jacket around my shoulders. The only thing lacking was a ring for my finger and a fatted calf.

The prodigal had returned. I was so glad to be home.

"I don't deserve this," I choked out. They waved off my comment. I wanted to tell them how dark and desperate my experience had been. I wanted them to know how sorry I was for putting them through this ordeal. They didn't want to discuss it—not then and not ever.

> "I wanted to tell them how dark and desperate my experience had been. I wanted them to know how sorry I was for putting them through this ordeal."

It was mid-December, so I was just in time for Christmas. While in prison, I had an overpowering feeling that I had looked at death up close. I was sure I was not going to come out of that situation alive. And now, I was home for the holidays, just like in the song.

Although I didn't make it home for Thanksgiving, there was nothing I wasn't thankful for. I sat, reflected, and praised God for hours. He had stopped me in my tracks in Mexico, and I was so grateful. As I reflected on all that had happened, I decided Romans 6:23

summed up the biggest lesson I'd learned: "For sin pays its wage—death; but God's free gift is eternal life in union with Christ Jesus our Lord" (GNT).

Knowing I was eager to get back on my feet, my very supportive brother gave me a job lead. A construction company Bill knew of had openings, and they hired me to install pipelines for $20 an hour. It was a tremendous amount of money for a nineteen-year-old to be making in 1973. Sure, digging ditches to bury pipelines was hard work, but I loved every minute! The job lasted two months, until the ground froze in February, just long enough for me to get into an apartment, repair my car, and put away some savings. When the construction crew took off to Florida until the ground thawed in New York, I stayed to find more work at home. I couldn't accept a government handout, like my buddies were going to do, when I was capable of working.

> ". . . I realized that if I didn't make some new —and very different— connections, I'd land right back in a world of hurt."

I reconnected with some old friends, and that almost led to another downfall. I had been in prison, which made me kind of a rock star in their eyes. I have to admit, the notoriety felt pretty good. But after a close brush with the law at a rock concert I attended with these former buddies, I realized that if I didn't make some new—and very different—connections, I'd land right back in a world of hurt.

The Yellow Pages listed plenty of options for churches. I visited a Presbyterian church one Sunday, an Episcopal congregation the next, then a Baptist gathering. I particularly enjoyed worshipping with believers at a black Pentecostal church. Finally, Karen suggested her wonderful, Bible-centered church in Schenectady. It was a perfect fit.

I also landed a full-time job as a salesman for Hahn's Shoes at the new, upscale Colonie Center Mall in Albany. Right in front of Hahn's door was a photo kiosk where five young women snapped pictures of children, all day long. I got to know the photographers.

The Language of Freedom

Paul and Raul introduced me to Jesus through the pages of Scripture, and then the guard opened the door of the prison and gestured me outside. There was no hesitation in my step. He had shown me the way out of that awful place, and I was only too glad to make my exit.

Time and time again in the last four decades of walking with Christ, I have seen a similar thing happen in the lives of men and women all over the world, when they first hear the Word of God in their own language and realize that they, too, have just been shown the way to freedom. I have been privileged to hear songs and shouts of joy in dozens of languages and on almost every continent.

It happened recently, when my wife, Rita, and I were privileged to worship with believers in Yunnan Province, in southwestern China. Many of us in the western world tend to think of China as a single, massive, monolingual entity; we conceive of this nation of more than a billion people as having some sort of homogenized, "Chinese" identity, culture, and even language. But this notion could hardly be further from the truth; China is a land of astounding diversity. This is especially true in Yunnan Province, home to more ethnic minority groups than any other province in China. Some fifteen languages are spoken here—in addition to "official" Mandarin Chinese—and many of these have multiple subdialects in everyday use.

For Christian believers like ninety-one-year-old Wang Xiufang, this means that finding a Bible to read can be very difficult. Wang starts every day by sitting on her front porch and opening her large, well-used Bible for her daily reading. But for many of her neighbors—especially those in the more rural areas that characterize much of this mountainous region, dominated by various forms of agriculture—a Bible in the primary language of the area is nonexistent.

Since 2000, the American Bible Society has been partnering with the church in China to translate the Scriptures into seven of the minority languages spoken by 85 percent of Yunnan's 800,000 Christians. For those of us accustomed to the easy availability of Bibles in our own languages, it may be tempting to ask, "Why not just translate into the languages spoken by the majority—Mandarin, for example—and let that suffice?"

The answer is eloquently provided by Ng Hwee Hong, program coordinator for the Bible translation partnership for Yunnan: "When minority people groups hear the Bible in Mandarin, it's as though a teacher is speaking to them. But when they hear the Bible in their own tongue, it's as though their mother and father are speaking to them."[1]

Let that idea soak in for a moment: the difference between the voice of a teacher or lecturer and the voice of a beloved parent. If you were trapped in a cycle of poverty, illiteracy, and spiritual disorientation, which voice would you be more inclined to listen to?

1. Jack Newman, "China's Mountain Church," *American Bible Society Record*, Spring 2016, 14.

And it's important to note how intimately related Bible translation is to increasing literacy rates in underprivileged parts of the world. In Yunnan, for example, Scripture-based literacy classes, sponsored by Bible translation ministry partners, help children learn to read the stories of the Bible in their own languages, as recently demonstrated by the successful launch of the New Testament in the White Yi language spoken by about 60,000 Christians in Yunnan.

Local church leader Li Wangsan said, "The church can use [the New Testament] to teach our young people the language. Our children are coming to church after they finish school in the afternoon to learn to read the White Yi language."[2]

In fact, it is remarkable to reflect on how often the Bible's entry into a previously unreached area is the precursor to an inflow of ministry to the illiterate, to children, to the sick, and to people with all

> ". . . it is remarkable to reflect on how often the Bible's entry into a previously unreached area is the precursor to an inflow of ministry to the illiterate, to children, to the sick, and to people with all sorts of other needs. When you think about it, it makes sense; once God's Word begins to transform us from the inside out, we want to spread the gift around— to do all we can to show God's love to the hurting world around us."

2. Newman, 18.

sorts of other needs. When you think about it, it makes sense; once God's Word begins to transform us from the inside out, we want to spread the gift around—to do all we can to show God's love to the hurting world around us.

In Yunnan Province, as a next step, the Bible Society partnership is commissioning local preachers and providing them with motorcycles to make the difficult journey into the mountainous rural terrain in order to reach rural villages with the message of hope—opening the door that leads out of prison and into the fresh air of freedom.

The Fleshpots of Egypt

But sadly, some people would rather stay in prison than live free. It's hard to believe, but it is really true. In Mexico, I met men who would intentionally get arrested so they could get into prison for a place to sleep and three meals a day. Life in prison was better than their life outside.

One of the saddest passages in the Bible is found in Exodus 16. At this point, Moses has led the Israelite people out of the land of bondage. God has miraculously delivered them from the sword of Pharaoh by parting the Red Sea and then closing it behind them, cutting off the pursuit of the Egyptian armies. Not only that, but He has miraculously provided safe water for them to drink (Exodus 15:25). Despite all the mighty works of God that they have witnessed, however, the people grouched and complained as they walked through the desert toward the freedom of the Promised Land. And then, in Exodus 16:2, we read this astounding statement: "There in the desert they all complained to Moses and Aaron and said to them, 'We wish that the LORD had killed us in Egypt. There we could at least sit down and eat meat and as much other food as we wanted. But you have brought us out into this desert to starve us all to death" (GNT).

Talk about selective memory! Apparently, the Israelites had not only forgotten about the miraculous deliverance they had recently received; they had also forgotten a few things about the harsh life imposed on them during their Egyptian slavery. For example, in order to control their population, Pharaoh had made the decree that all Israelite boys had to be killed at birth. Also, there was that difficult business about making bricks without the straw necessary to provide the binding material. Life in Egypt for the Israelite people had been about as far from a bed of roses as you can get!

> ". . . too many people are enslaved and imprisoned—of their own free will! They would rather stay in a dark jail of their own making than live in the freedom and light that God offers them through His Word."

And yet, now they are saying to Moses, in effect, "What are we doing in this desert? Why can't we go back to the good old days in Egypt?"

This story saddens me because it reminds me that too many people are enslaved and imprisoned—of their own free will! They would rather stay in a dark jail of their own making than live in the freedom and light that God offers them through His Word.

It has been said that there are none so blind as those who will not see; the saddest situation is when we choose to ignore what we already know. Or, as Jeremiah describes it, "foolish and stupid people, who have eyes, but cannot see, and have ears, but cannot hear" (Jeremiah 5:21, GNT). And in our Bible-rich nation, with churches on countless street corners, this problem has never been greater.

In 2007, the president of the Barna Group and the founder of Q Ideas released the results of their research on attitudes toward the church on the part of Americans ages sixteen to twenty-nine In *UnChristian: What a New Generation Really Thinks about Christianity . . . and Why It Matters*, they reveal that a substantial number of these individuals view Christians and the church in a very negative light. In fact, according to Kinnaman and Lyons, only about one in seven Americans has a positive view of the Christian faith— and this includes people who grew up in the church![3]

> "When kids see their parents, church leaders, and other religious authority figures acting disrespectfully toward each other, attacking persons they do not understand or agree with, taking advantage of those in their pastoral care, and displaying other traits that are utterly foreign to the way Jesus treated people, it is no wonder that they conclude that 'church people' are 'literalistic, anti-intellectual, self-righteous, judgmental, and bigoted.'"

3. David Kinnaman and Gabe Lyons, *UnChristian: What a New Generation Really Thinks about Christianity . . . and Why It Matters* (Ada, MI: Baker Books, 2007).

We must admit, with deep sadness, that the actions, attitudes, and practices of those of us in the church deserve a large proportion of the blame for this situation. When kids see their parents, church leaders, and other religious authority figures acting disrespectfully toward each other, attacking persons they do not understand or agree with, taking advantage of those in their pastoral care, and displaying other traits that are utterly foreign to the way Jesus treated people, it is no wonder that they conclude that "church people" are "literalistic, anti-intellectual, self-righteous, judgmental, and bigoted."[4]

Clearly, skepticism toward Christianity is on the rise in America, and the church must meet this challenge. I believe that the number-one antidote to a skeptical public that is mistrustful of the church is an authentic encounter with Jesus as He presents Himself in the Bible.

Philadelphia Freedom

Philadelphia, where Rita and I live and where American Bible Society has just relocated its headquarters, is often viewed as the cradle of American freedom. This makes sense when you consider that this is the place where the Continental Congress met and discussed the issues that ultimately led to the American Revolution; where the Declaration of Independence was signed; where the United States Constitution was debated and drafted, where the first English Bible was printed in the United States ... and where the original Liberty Bell first rang

4. Marcus Borg, *The Heart of Christianity: Rediscovering a Life of Faith* (San Francisco: HarperOne, 2004).

out! It is an amazing feeling to stand inside Independence Hall, looking at the desks and chairs where Benjamin Franklin, Thomas Jefferson, John Adams, George Washington, John Jay, and other visionary leaders of the Thirteen Colonies worked, wrote, argued, and compromised in order to hammer out the founding principles of our nation.

> "... the story of American freedom is incomplete without proper consideration of the role of the Bible in our free society. The Bible is one of the sources, one of the foundational documents that drove these farsighted thinkers and propelled their notions of what constituted a free, democratic society."

But the story of American freedom is incomplete without proper consideration of the role of the Bible in our free society. The Bible is one of the sources, one of the foundational documents that drove these farsighted thinkers and propelled their notions of what constituted a free, democratic society. In later years, the Bible would provide much of the impetus for the anti-slavery movement that would agitate tirelessly for the liberation of all people. From the first day of our nation until now, the Bible has occupied the hearts and minds that have shaped and guided America's place in the world.

This is why American Bible Society, as an integral part of its move to its new home, located on the Independence Mall, just steps from historic Independence Hall, plans to open a state-of-the-art Faith and Liberty Discovery Center. This exciting new facility will offer hands-on, interactive, intellectually and spiritually rich opportunities for Bible engagement to visitors, travelers, and Philadelphia residents alike. In our effort to offer all a chance to have an open encounter with Jesus Christ, we are pulling out all the stops in order to present Scripture to our twenty-first-century culture in a way that is relevant, truth-filled, and engaging.[5]

Our passion for introducing people to the living God of Scripture is also what motivated us to partner in a major media production, *The Passion*, a musical that aired on a major television network during Passion Week, 2016. Including 360-degree videos and Bible-based character profiles, this effort also integrated family discussion guides and materials for churches and small-group Bible study.[6]

Similarly, American Bible Society has led the way in building a Digital Bible Library of all Scripture available globally. This has provided access for partners like YouVersion, which is now the most downloaded Bible app in the world.

We are doing this as a part of our all-in focus to invite everyone to encounter the life-changing Scriptures. Today, we face an American public that is increasingly alienated from Christianity. Thousands upon thousands of people in this country are sitting in a

5. "American Bible Society Is Making Its New Home in Historic Philadelphia." Nic.Bible blog, American Bible Society [online]. Available at http://www.nic.bible /blog/post/american-bible-society-is-making-its-new-home-in-historic-philadelphia#. V1SiIFdfvO8 (accessed June 5, 2016).

6. "American Bible Society Brings Viewers inside the Passion Experience." *American Bible Society News*, March 8, 2016 [online]. Available at http://news.american bible.org/blog/entry/corporate-blog/american-bible-society-brings-viewers-inside-the -passion-experience (accessed June 5, 2016).

prison they have fashioned for themselves, and they will not walk through the open door to be set free.

> "We will try every approach, embrace every new technology, pursue every viable delivery system, and exhaust every possibility in our efforts to introduce people everywhere to the words of the God who saves."

Those of us who love God and have experienced the liberation He provides cannot accept this. We will try every approach, embrace every new technology, pursue every viable delivery system, and exhaust every possibility in our efforts to introduce people everywhere to the words of the God who saves. People are in bondage—whether they realize it or not. We cannot rest until they are free.

Food for Thought

- God's love and mercy deliver us from bondage: "There is no condemnation now for those who live in union with Christ Jesus" (Romans 8:1, GNT).

- While people have been shown the way to freedom through hearing the Word of God in their own language, many would rather stay in prison than live free.

- Those of us who have experienced God's liberation will do all we can to share that freedom with others.

Questions to Consider

1. What events in your life are you eager to put behind you? What would it take to receive God's mercy and be set free?

2. Imagine hearing the Bible read by a beloved parent, or friend. How does this change your experience? How does it impact your understanding?

3. How have your experiences in the church and with Christianity shaped your perception of the Bible? Have any of these experiences created obstacles in hearing God's Word speak to you?

Chapter 5

WHAT SELLING SHOES TAUGHT ME ABOUT LIFE

I alone know the plans I have for you,
plans to bring you prosperity and not disaster,
plans to bring about the future you hope for.

Jeremiah 29:11 (GNT)

H er name was Rita; I found that out pretty quickly. In between her photography appointments and when things weren't too busy at my shoe store, we started talking. Before too long, we were having lunch together. Not long after that, we were going to the movies or just spending time together.

She captivated me immediately. Rita was—and still is—a beautiful woman with a beautiful spirit. She was so easy to talk to, and she seemed to really listen—as though she honestly wanted to know all the details of my experience in Mexico and my life. I felt safe opening up to her, and we soon became good friends.

My work was going well, too. After a few months on the job, the Hahn's district manager greeted me as I walked into the store one day. "The manager and assistant manager are gone," he said. "They've been stealing from us."

I was shocked! And then I realized that just a year before, I could easily have been involved in their schemes. Now I handled thousands of dollars a day, and every penny, every dollar, every pair of shoes was accounted for.

The district manager offered me a promotion to assistant manager. I was astounded; this was definitely a blessing from God.

I was willing to work six days a week, twelve hours a day. I would have slept in the back of the store if they'd asked me. Work was a joy! Inventories balanced, losses went down, and sales went up.

Almost by the day, I felt as if I were changing. God's Word was transforming my life; the more I read my Bible, the more I wanted to read it.

Rita was puzzled by this; it seemed like an obsession to her. And honestly, I didn't fully understand it, either. But there were three things I knew for sure: I loved God, I loved His Word, and I was falling in love with Rita.

As I had learned, Rita brought her own set of challenging circumstances to the mix. When we met, she was a single mom with a two-year-old son named Dean. She had been dating someone else when we met.

At first, all she wanted was to be friends. We would go out to dinner, talk endlessly, and laugh a lot. Then I would drive her home. For Rita, this was comfortable; it was all she was really looking for at that time.

Then, one crisp fall evening, when we left a restaurant and walked to the car, I did something I hadn't planned and that she didn't expect: as I opened her door, I leaned over and kissed her.

On the way home, the car was pretty quiet. That kiss—which I had been yearning to do for months—changed everything. Rita was wondering if she had just lost the friend she was coming to value so much. And I was wondering if I had just blown my friendship with the most wonderful woman I had ever met.

The next time Rita's boyfriend came back from law school in Boston to visit her, I took what some might consider an unusual step; I invited him for dinner—just the two of us. I really wanted to talk to him, because Rita was becoming very important to me, and I wanted to let him know that. If she was as important to him as she was to me, then, I guess I would have to learn to live with it. But at least everything would be out on the table.

It may sound strange, but we really hit it off! He was a good guy, and best of all, he really seemed to understand and respect where I was coming from with Rita. By the time we finished our visit, he said, "Roy, you are the better man for Rita." He even agreed to tell her himself!

But despite this, Rita still wasn't ready for a serious relationship with me, or with anyone else. The pain of her broken marriage was still too fresh. We kept on seeing each other, and I really was coming to think the world of Dean. He seemed to like me, too.

I decided to take the plunge. On New Year's Eve, after Rita had put Dean to bed, she came back into the living room of her house. I was waiting for her with a ring in my pocket. I took it out, opened the box, and showed it to her. "Will you marry me, Rita?" I asked. She seemed so surprised, stunned . . . and not in a good way. This was not going well.

"No, Roy, I can't," she said.

I felt like someone had punched me in the stomach, but I kept my composure. "Well, then, will you just keep the ring over the weekend and think about it?" She agreed to this, but on Monday morning it was as if she could hardly wait to give it back to me.

Either I am a very slow learner or I just don't know when to give up; I prefer to think it is the latter. I exchanged the diamond engagement ring for a beautiful gold and coral ring and gave it to Rita a few days later. "Will you accept this as a gift?" I said. She took the ring as a sign of friendship and agreed to wear it. But in the back of my mind, I still felt engaged to Rita.

After that, things became kind of strained between us. It makes sense, looking back; I was in one place emotionally, and she was in another, for good reason. But that didn't make it easier at the time.

Moving On, Moving Up

During my second year with Hahn's, I was promoted to manager of a store in Philadelphia. At that time, I was twenty-one years old. "Grow a mustache or something," my supervisor said. "You look like a stock boy." I grew the mustache and made the move. I felt stung by Rita's refusal, and I have to admit, it felt good to move away and to receive the approval of my employer in the form of a promotion, more money, and more responsibility.

When I wasn't managing the Hahn's store at the King of Prussia Mall, I was studying my Bible or attending a church. Finally, I settled in at a great church in downtown Philadelphia, under the leadership of Dr. James Montgomery Boice. I grew tremendously under his teaching. Every time the doors opened, I was there. Attending a Bible study during the week also became part of my routine. My life was full, busy, and I was growing.

Then Rita came to visit. It had been a few months, and I was excited to see her. After picking her up at the airport, I took her out for a nice, quiet dinner.

"Roy, I have been thinking," she said. "I really do love you and I've changed my mind. I will marry you."

But while Rita was becoming ready to move forward, I had been learning what God's Word had to say about marriage. Second Corinthians 6:14 said, "Do not try to work together as equals with unbelievers, for it cannot be done. How can right and wrong be partners? How can light and darkness live together?" (GNT). I didn't think Rita could understand this. I wasn't sure Rita was even saved, and I still didn't know how to talk to someone about receiving Christ as her Savior.

I loved Rita, so it broke my heart to say, "Rita, I'm so sorry, but I can't marry you."

"Is there someone else in your life?" she asked.

The "Someone" was Jesus. I was doing my best to obey His every commandment. But how could I tell her that the person standing in the way of our relationship was Jesus?

"Roy, do you still love me?"

"Yes, I do. But I've changed."

"I can see that, Roy. We used to go out and have fun; now you just want to stay home and read the Bible."

She wasn't wrong. And I didn't have the words to explain it to her very well.

She went back to New York feeling hurt and rejected—very similar to the way I had felt when I moved to Philadelphia. But once again, God had something unexpected and amazing in store.

Focusing on the Goal

Day by day, I was gaining more and more confidence in myself in my new leadership and management responsibilities. I was doing a good job for Hahn's, and they were noticing. I was energetic, dedicated, honest, grateful for the opportunities I was receiving, and above all, I was focused on doing things the right way. I had come a long way from the day I left home for southern California in search of freedom and a good time. Without a doubt, the changes God's Word was making in my heart were also contributing to my success in my newfound career.

Good focus is vital to accomplishing almost anything of importance. This was hammered home to me, not only during my career in business, but later when, as the leader of a worldwide Bible translation organization, I was brought face-to-face with one of the most important challenges—and opportunities—the Bible translation movement has ever faced.

Around 2011, a group of concerned, deeply committed Christian entrepreneurs and philanthropists made a provocative observation: too many of us in the Bible movement were working in silos. In other words, each of us was so preoccupied with our own efforts at translating, publishing, or distributing Bibles around the world that we were ignoring the possibilities for cooperation and collaboration. "You are so busy doing the work," they told us, "that you're missing an opportunity to accomplish the goal. Your individual efforts are wasting time and money."

The more we looked at what they were saying, the more we began to realize they were right. Driven by the astounding pace of change in digital publishing and distribution capabilities, an opportunity existed to form strategic alliances that would permit us to actually deliver what we each said was our ultimate intention: access to the Bible for every person on earth. Our focus was right, but getting there would take a whole new way of working together.

> "Driven by the astounding pace of change in digital publishing and distribution capabilities, an opportunity existed to form strategic alliances that would permit us to actually deliver what we each said was our ultimate intention: access to the Bible for every person on earth."

In December 2012, the "Every Tribe Every Nation" (ETEN) initiative was launched as a partnership among Biblica (International Bible Society), Wycliffe Bible Translators USA, The Seed Company, SIL International (formerly Summer Institute of Linguistics, Inc.), and American Bible Society. Our vision was to leverage the individual strengths of our organizations in ways that would accelerate the pace of Bible translation and distribution to the remaining language groups in the world that had no Scripture available to them. The objective is to provide Bible access to "every tribe and every nation" in the world by the year 2033.[1]

---

1. "World's Three Major Bible Ministries Partner with Philanthropists to Create The Digital Bible Library" (press release), Every Tribe Every Nation, December 13, 2012. Available at http://www.everytribeeverynation.org/Websites/eten/files/Content/4096494/etendbllaunch-releasefinal.pdf (accessed June 7, 2016).

The centerpiece of this effort was the formation of The Digital Bible Library, housed and operated by United Bible Societies, the international association of Bible societies of which American Bible Society is a founding member. This centralized biblical database provides an efficient and seamless platform for Bible translations in all languages to be standardized, digitized, centralized, and accredited. These texts are then made available to vetted Christian organizations, ministries, and missionaries, much in the same way as checking a book out of a library. Never has it been so easy for God's Word to be made available—efficiently, accurately, and almost instantly—to so many people in so many different languages. And at the same time, the translators' intellectual property is respected and protected.

In retrospect, the concept seems so simple, like most really great ideas. We just needed to shift our focus from translation, production, and distribution to full access to the Bible— the core principle that each of our organizations was founded upon in the first place.

This momentous strategic shift in focus to full and digital access has made possible what is perhaps the most important development in Bible translation and distribution since Gutenberg invented the printing press in the fifteenth century. I honestly do not believe that is an exaggeration. And visionary financial partners and developers seem to agree. Thanks to their efforts, 2,000 versions of Scripture are expected to be ready for digital access by 2017.

Engaging the Heart

With the astounding, worldwide growth in the use of mobile phone technology—even in the developing world—The Digital Bible

Library and the associated efforts of the ETEN initiative hold tremendous promise as a tool for reaching unprecedented numbers of people still living in biblical poverty. But technology is not the be-all and end-all. Technology makes some things easier, quicker, and more accurate, but it cannot, by itself, accomplish the most critical task of all: engaging human hearts with the living, active Word of God. For that, we still need people.

We need people like Morgan Jackson, for example. Since 1972, when Morgan's parents, Jerry and Anet Jackson, began recording the Bible in the Hopi language, their ministry, Faith Comes by Hearing (taken from the words of Romans 10:17), has been a pioneer in providing audio Scripture in the languages of the world's many primarily oral cultures. Morgan has a trove of stories about the amazing transformations he has witnessed when people hear the Word of God spoken aloud in their local dialects.

> "Technology makes some things easier, quicker, and more accurate, but it cannot, by itself, accomplish the most critical task of all: engaging human hearts with the living, active Word of God. For that, we still need people."

Morgan is also someone well acquainted with the advantages of technology. They have developed and distributed audio Bibles in almost every digital and analog format you can name, starting with the cassettes his parents handed out on the Hopi reservation back in the 1970s. Today, Morgan utilizes everything from solar-powered digital audio "Proclaimers" that can be operated deep in the bush, far from any electrical grid, to mp3s and "Bible Sticks":

matchbook-sized audio players preloaded with the complete New Testament. He has seen the spoken Word engage hearts and lives in places as diverse as Ghana and Guatemala. And in every case, it was the human connection that made it possible for the technology to reach its target.

> "The goal of reaching everyone in the world with the Bible in his or her heart language has never been more attainable."

The goal of reaching everyone in the world with the Bible in his or her heart language has never been more attainable. But in order to realize that, we needed to change our focus. We also need more people of vision, dedicated to making the Bible accessible to everyone, everywhere; and then to empowering those people to engage the Word of God with their minds and hearts.

Food for Thought

- Good focus is vital to accomplishing almost anything of importance.

- In order to achieve your goals, you may need to shift your focus.

- The goal of reaching everyone in the world with the Bible in his or her heart language has never been more attainable, but in order to accomplish this, we need the right focus and more people committed to carrying out the work.

Questions to Consider

1. Have you ever had to give up something important in order to follow God? How did it make you feel? What was the result of your decision?

2. Is there a particular goal that you are focused on right now? What will it take to reach your goal? Does this goal line up with your most important priorities in life?

3. What partnerships have helped further your goals? What skills, vision, or support did these partnerships offer? How have these partnerships impacted others?

Chapter 6

IN LOVE WITH AN ITALIAN PHOTOGRAPHER

There is no more lovely, friendly, or charming relation-
ship, communion, or company, than a good marriage.

Martin Luther

S truggling with getting through life as a single mom, and confused by my response to her, one day Rita was invited to a
church service by, of all people, the mail carrier at work. Rita said
it seemed like a miracle when she asked her boss for the evening
off and he gave it to her. But that was only the first miracle. The
second was that she actually went to the church, and the third, she
said, was that she found it (she has never claimed a sense of direction
as her strong suit). But the fourth and greatest miracle, she said, is
that when she heard the Gospel message that night, she really heard
it in a way that she had never experienced before.

When an invitation to make a personal move of faith came, she
practically ran to the front. The people at that church wrapped their
arms and their hearts around her. They prayed with her according
to Romans 10:9–10: "If you confess that Jesus is Lord and believe
that God raised him from death, you will be saved. For it is by our

faith that we are put right with God; it is by our confession that we are saved" (GNT). For Rita, it was as if God had also wrapped His arms around her, along with the people at the church. She cried all the way back to her house. She could hardly wait to tell me what had happened.

Drunk on Jesus!

As I answered the phone in my room in Philadelphia, I had no idea what was about to happen.

"Roy," Rita said softly, "I've been to church . . ." Her voice trembled with excitement and joy. "I feel like I'm drunk on Jesus!" she said. And she really was. This was what I'd been praying for! I asked her a number of questions to understand what had happened.

"Rita, now we can get married!" I said. As Rita tells it, she "got saved and engaged on the same night." We set a wedding date for Sunday, June 13, 1976. Here we were: two broken people with broken pasts, two college dropouts, but life had started falling into place for us.

Right before our wedding, the US Shoe Corporation, parent company for Hahn's, offered me a management position back in New York, in a store located just northwest of Manhattan. It was another amazing promotion. I took it.

On June 13, I stood at the altar, watching the four-year-old, curly haired Dean march down the aisle, dressed in his little shorts, dress shirt, and bow tie. His big smile grabbed at my heart. Then Rita walked toward me. Wow! Her blue eyes glistened. She was radiant, beautiful, and deeply in love with God and with me. What more could a man ask for? God poured out His richest blessings on my life that day.

Just a little over a year later, in the winter of 1978, Rita and I were baptized together. Rita was now pregnant with our son Wesley. We've often noted that Wes was baptized twice: once when Rita was carrying him, and later in life, as a young man at our church in Florida. Jordan went forward in the early 1990s to be baptized at our church in Quito, Ecuador. I had the joy of baptizing our daughter, Corrie, while home on furlough at our church in Florida.

We joined a great church in Nanuet, New York, and settled in. The pastor, Dr. Leslie Flynn, is one of the finest Bible teachers I've ever heard. For the next seven years, Rita and I established a firm foundation in the faith under his leadership.

We both taught Sunday school, where we learned right along with the kids. Rita became the church photographer, and she was involved in women's ministry. We were members of a good church, and we were happy.

Meanwhile, my new promotion had taken us to one of the most expensive places in the country, just outside New York City, so although I had a good job, it didn't make ends meet. Rita's photography skills helped keep us afloat. Amazingly, God was opening doors for us, and we were able to buy a home for our second Christmas together. We felt blessed beyond our wildest dreams!

Life was good. And it got even better when I was offered a management position with Florsheim Shoes, where I would be responsible for merchandise purchasing and overseeing the staff of a growing new store. This huge step in my young career kept me working night and day.

The Trouble with Success

The only problem was that, little by little, it was taking a toll on my family life. By 1980, Dean now had two brothers, Wesley and Jordan. It was always an emotional struggle, wanting to be with my family more while balancing the demands of work. With three boys—one still in diapers—Rita had her hands full. She was juggling many responsibilities while caring for our boys and home, teaching Sunday school, being involved in a couple's group, and at the same time growing her photography business.

One Sunday morning, I found out just how hard things were for her. Exhausted from my sixty-hour week, I was reading the paper while Rita was cleaning the kitchen, getting the boys dressed, and trying to get herself ready so we could all go to church. And then, for some reason, Jordan, who was only two years old, wouldn't put his coat on. It was the last straw.

"That's it! We're not going!" she said. Coats were flying; doors were slamming—and trust me when I tell you that we didn't customarily slam doors or throw things in our home. I put down the sports section. Rita had my full attention.

"You can't keep working so much that you have no energy when you *are* home!" she sobbed. "I need you *here!*" She ran into the bedroom and locked the door.

The boys and I looked at each other. I wrestled them into their coats, scooped them up, and put them in the car. I prayed all the way to church. After dropping the boys off at Sunday school, I turned around and drove back home as fast as I dared.

My wife was literally exhausted, and I wasn't helping. Time and again I'd promised Rita that I'd lighten my workload and be home more. But I hadn't followed through; the business I was building was really growing. There was always another challenge right around the corner, another chance to advance, to meet the demands of a successful business.

But no position, no amount of money, *nothing* was worth losing my family. I had to face the uncomfortable realization that my priorities were out of order.

I was ready to change anything, everything, to save my family. When I got home, the bedroom door was still locked and Rita was still crying. I knocked—gently.

> "But no position, no amount of money, *nothing* was worth losing my family."

"I can't do this anymore," she said.

"Rita, I am so sorry. I *promise* I will get another job."

She finally believed me and unlocked the door. I grabbed her in my arms and hugged her tight before I raced back out the door to pick up the boys from Sunday school.

That same evening, I opened the paper and scanned the *New York Times* classifieds. A wholesale marketing position with American Greetings Corporation seemed to leap off the page.

I made a call that resulted in a meeting with the district manager in New Jersey that week. When we sat down at a table across from one another, the man said to me, "I want you to sell me something."

Pulling out a rosewood pen and pencil set from my suit pocket—a set, by the way, made by Hallmark, the company that happened to be American Greetings' biggest competition—I sold the executive these pens. He hired me on the spot.

I was no longer in the shoe business. Instead, I was in the greeting card business as a regional sales rep. It was a Monday-through-Friday, nine-to-five job—and a big financial step down. But that didn't matter; I was home every night and weekend with my wife and three boys. For the next seven years, I worked for American Greetings.

The company moved us to Rhode Island in 1982. After I received two promotions, Rita and I had a home overlooking Narragansett Bay, with two new cars in the driveway. The boys were in private school, and Rita no longer had to work outside the home. Once again, God was blessing us beyond our wildest dreams.

Life Is a Journey

I can honestly say that Rita and I are more in love with each other today than we have ever been, but it has not been a steady, upward pattern. As in any relationship, we've had our good days and our bad days—and our good months and bad months. But through all of that, we have managed, by the grace and strength of God, to keep trusting each other, to continue respecting each other, and to maintain honest communication with each other. There is no human being more important to me in my journey through life than my beloved wife.

It is the same with each of us and our relationship with God. Especially in the early days, when I was just discovering faith, I was infatuated with the Bible and with God, like a lovestruck kid with his first crush. Over the years, as I have continued to learn, mature, and experience the many ups and downs of life on this earth, my faith in God and daily trust in Him has grown. It has become more discerning, more patient, more multifaceted.

Now, don't misunderstand me: God has not changed! From day one until now, He has loved me, watched over me, and guided my feet along the way He intended for me to go. He has also been deeply patient and loving with me, His sometimes-impetuous and often-impatient child. But as I have continued along the way, I am the one who has been changed: transformed more and more into something resembling His glory, as I seek diligently to walk the path He is providing. To paraphrase Paul in 2 Corinthians 3:18, the more I keep my eyes on God, the more I start to look like Him—not because I'm a good imitator, but because God is the ultimate makeover artist.

> ". . . the more I keep my eyes on God, the more I start to look like Him—not because I'm a good imitator, but because God is the ultimate makeover artist."

Gaining a Heart for the Lost

Living and working in New England as members of a great church, we continued growing in faith under the mentorship of Dr. David Madeira. As we became more involved in the church, we met Dr. and Mrs. Howard Ferrin. Dr. Ferrin was the founder and president of Barrington Christian College, and his wife, Evelyn, saw something in us we didn't see at the time.

"Young man, you're twenty-nine years old," she said to me. "You should be involved in missions!"

So I signed up for the missions committee. I dove into learning everything I could about it. Rita and I began praying for the unreached peoples of the world. I studied the missions budget and the organizations we supported. I wanted to have all the information in good order so we could be wise stewards of our outreach resources. When Mrs. Ferrin rotated off the missions committee as chair, they elected me to take her place.

> "... when people receive God's Word in their language, they think, *You mean our language is valuable? Is it possible that God loves us as much as He loves people from cultures*"

As I studied missions, I discovered that many people groups have a diminished view of themselves and feel unworthy of God because of their language and culture. Coming from a dominant, powerful nation, we Americans have a hard time grasping the marginalization that takes place in other cultures. Due to poverty and lack of education, many ethnic, cultural, and linguistic minorities are looked down upon by other larger and more powerful populations.

I was shocked to learn that many languages don't even have an alphabet! In these areas, people see themselves as having no value. They think, *if we were worth anything, we would have a dictionary, an alphabet, a newspaper, schools, right?*

But when people receive God's Word in their language, they think, *You mean our language is valuable? Is it possible that God loves*

us as much as He loves people from cultures that have universities?
And when they find out that God sent His Son on their behalf, the
impact is staggering.

In 1982, approximately half the nearly 7,000 languages did not
have an alphabet or any written materials in their language, and
without God's Word in their mother tongue, they didn't know that
God spoke their language! Although we have made significant progress since that time, today there are still over 1,600 languages that
don't have even one verse of Scripture. Fewer than 600 languages
have the entire Bible. Clearly, there is still much work to be done
to complete the task Jesus gave the Church when he told us to take
the Good News to all nations (Matthew 28:19–20, GNT).

I didn't fully realize it then, but God was instilling in my heart
a longing for those who had never heard the Gospel—and especially those who had never heard it in their own language. Little by
little, He was creating in me a place of "divine discontent," as Ralph
Waldo Emerson called it. He was planting in my heart a seed that
would one day blossom into a full-blown passion for ending "Bible
poverty" throughout the world.

Food for Thought

- Sometimes we need to reevaluate our priorities; nothing is worth losing our families over.

- While we face peaks and valleys in our spiritual lives, we are continually being formed into God's likeness.

- "Divine discontent" can indicate a way God is stirring our hearts to meet a need in the world.

Questions to Consider

1. How would you rank your priorities right now? Is anything important being compromised that should get more attention or value?

2. Have you ever felt unworthy? What prompted this feeling? What would Scripture say to you about this feeling or situation?

3. Is there a ministry in your church or city God is stirring your heart to participate in? What skills could you contribute?

Chapter 7

THE GOOD LIFE

Faith never knows where it is being led,
but it loves and knows the One who is leading.

Oswald Chambers

I was surprisingly becoming more and more interested in working directly to fulfill Jesus' Great Commission. Like a divine accelerant, my desire for greater involvement in missions was stoked by a trip that Dean and I made to Haiti with our senior pastor and other church members in the early 1980s. We brought food, medical help, and the Gospel message to some of the poorest people in the Western Hemisphere. We planted trees, helped provide clean water, and offered vocational training.

While there, Dean and I experienced so many eye-opening moments. We saw firsthand the effects of voodoo, evil spirits, abject poverty, acute sickness, and pain. Dean and I realized the utter hopelessness of humanity without Christ. We treasured every minute we were able to serve the Haitian people. Bringing them hope and sharing God's Word with them was such a privilege.

Rita had stayed home with Wes and Jordan, the two younger boys. She could see the zeal in our faces as Dean and I told her about what we had witnessed in Haiti. She could also sense the deep desire in my heart—growing stronger each day—to go to a place in the world where the Gospel was little known in order to extend the reach of God's kingdom.

"I'm just not quite there yet," she told me, after one of our late-night talks about all that needed to be done to reach the lost. I respected her feelings, knowing that I should not override her honest misgivings in something involving such an irreversible commitment as going to the mission field.

Nevertheless, the desire in my heart just kept growing. Not long after Dean and I got back from Haiti, I received another promotion, and American Greetings moved us to the Tampa, Florida, area. Now as senior national account manager, I was responsible for greeting card sales to the national Eckerd Drugstore chain (now CVS Pharmacies), and I served their stores across fifteen states. But one day, when I had just made a $5 million sale and realized that I was more excited about our missions conference, I knew my days in the greeting card business were numbered.

About this time, Rita's dad passed away. We knew of a retreat that was being held for women dealing with grief, and I encouraged her to attend, offering to care for Dean, Wes, and Jordan. While she was there, alone with God, she heard herself speaking these words to Him: "I will go wherever you want: Africa, China . . . I will do whatever you call us to do."

As she did so, she said that God whispered into her heart, *Rita, you need to let go of everything.*

She came home and told me of this intimate, precious experience of God's presence. I was overwhelmed and also grateful. We decided to knock on a few doors to see what opportunities God might have in mind for us to pursue our blossoming passion for reaching the lost.

Knocking on the Right Door

We did the only thing we knew to do to become missionaries; we applied to our first missions agency. The reply was swift: "Sorry, Rita has been divorced." Next, we applied to a second missions board. "Oh, we see you dropped out of college," they said. "We want all our people to have college degrees." I don't think they even got to the prison part of my résumé. Door after door closed. *Maybe we're not supposed to be missionaries after all,* we thought.

We pressed on, determined to keep seeking God's will. We prayed and we gave and we served where we could. We hungered to know God more. We wanted to give Him more of ourselves. We'd been taught to tithe and to give above the tithe.

> "We prayed and we gave and we served where we could. We hungered to know God more. We wanted to give Him more of ourselves. We'd been taught to tithe and to give above the tithe."

We were particularly drawn to supporting Wycliffe Bible Translators. Their vision and the work they did to take God's Word to unreached people groups resonated with us. We read all the material we received from them. One day, an article in the Wycliffe magazine caught my eye.

"Rita, listen to this: Wycliffe needs people with business management experience, and they need professional photographers." I said, "This sounds like us!" We didn't want to get our hopes up only to have them dashed to pieces again, but I was excited.

As a critical thinker, Rita ponders things and counts the cost. When she lands on a decision and is confident in her heart, she's full speed ahead in faith. I'm more spontaneous and optimistic. I can make a snap decision and run with it. Together we make a great team: I grab her hand and we leap, but not before she is sure we will land safely.

I was saying, "God's going to do a miracle!" Meanwhile, Rita was thinking, *Wycliffe's not going to accept us with our backgrounds, but there's no harm in filling out the application. If they turn us down, Roy will get this out of his system.* So we made the leap together, but with very different expectations.

> **"We had seen God take our two broken lives and restore us. We offered ourselves to Him for His exclusive service."**

I completed the application. We prayed, put a postage stamp on it, and mailed it. We took the risk. We had seen God take our two broken lives and restore us. We offered ourselves to Him for His exclusive service. Then we waited, frequently checking the mailbox.

The letter finally came in the fall of 1986. Wycliffe didn't say no—and they didn't say yes. They didn't mention college degrees, either. The interviewer seemed to think my business experience and Rita's photography samples were of similar value to college degrees. They did, however, notice the prison part of my résumé.

The letter noted, "Roy has been in prison, and Rita has been divorced. We need to know more about the circumstances of both."

Clarifying how Rita had honored all scriptural boundaries was easy. My vetting process, however, required a few more steps.

"Roy, you could be registered in Mexico [as a felon] and on a list in Washington, DC, which may make it difficult for you to get a passport and permission to live in some countries," they said.

Would our pasts pass the test? God had planted unreached people groups in our hearts; Rita and I had been praying over them for years. We needed Wycliffe as much as Wycliffe needed us.

Living inside a Miracle

Wycliffe hired the best investigator they could find and sent him to Ensenada, Mexico. A police detective and hostage negotiator from California, he left no stone unturned. He started in Mexico at the local level, then moved on to state and federal. Then he made inquiries in Washington, DC.

In the meantime, they sent us to North Carolina for an intensive, four-week training session for missionaries. The course was perfect for a college student without a family or job. We, however, were a family of six by that time, with our very supportive three sons and a beautiful new baby girl, Corrie (named after Corrie ten Boom; when she was three she would tell people her name was Corrie ten Boom Peterson). We were so excited to have a daughter. I was handling a multimillion-dollar national account, and I was now faced with asking my boss for four weeks off to train to possibly become a missionary. I knew such a request might put my job at risk, and I wasn't quite ready to "go public" yet. After all, Wycliffe still might not accept us.

My boss, Richard, was an atheist. He was also a very kind man who knew about my faith. I was meeting him at Atlanta airport for strategic planning when I gathered the courage to ask him for time off. He couldn't believe what he was hearing.

"Four weeks!" he said. "No one with your responsibility gets even two weeks off at one time. And you're asking for four?"

"Yes, Richard, I'm asking for four weeks."

He looked at me and said, "Does this have something to do with your God?"

"Yes, Richard, it has everything to do with my God."

"All right," he said, finally. "I will take your calls and cover for you. Please don't let anyone else know." I will always believe that God honored Richard for his support that day.

The trip to the facility in North Carolina was a defining moment for our entire family. All six of us were applying for this role. All of us fell in love with the movement and its mission to translate God's Word for every people group on earth. All of us were praying that by July 28, they would say, "You're in."

That didn't happen. Instead, the Petersons had to pack up and drive back to Tampa, still hoping and waiting for the investigator's findings. We arrived home in early August, and on the 15th we finally received a letter. Rita and I opened it together to read the investigator's findings.

"There's no evidence you were ever in Mexico, Roy." Not local, state, or federal. No record! And there are no issues from Washington, DC.

I was astounded—overcome with joy. I thought immediately of Psalm 103:12: "As far as the east is from the west; so far does he remove our sins from us" (GNT).

It was a time to rejoice, to weep at the magnitude of God's grace. I truly believed we were in the middle of a miracle! Joy, elation, and a Holy Spirit infusion flooded our emotions as we read, "Welcome to Wycliffe. Your journey is about to begin . . .

. . . and you'll be raising your own monthly salary support."

Gulp! Here we were, living in Florida in a wonderful home amid good neighbors, attending a great church, and enjoying the benefits of a fantastic salary—and we were about to pull up stakes, leave my job for one that didn't pay, sell everything we owned, and take four kids to the mission field. Oh, and by the way, at this point, only God knew our destination.

> "Here we were, living in Florida in a wonderful home amid good neighbors, attending a great church, and enjoying the benefits of a fantastic salary—and we were about to pull up stakes, leave my job for one that didn't pay, sell everything we owned, and take four kids to the mission field."

What were we thinking, exactly? We stared at the letter, then at each other.

Our Plans, God's Plan

Sometimes, as I think back on all I have seen during a career spent observing God's amazing provision, I have to shake my head and smile about all the times I have been surprised when the Lord does the marvelous and unexpected. You would think I would learn! But I must confess that I am continually caught off-guard by God's overflowing goodness to those who are trying faithfully to carry out His call in their lives.

I think my good friend Alexander Philip would agree.

Born in Nigeria to parents from South India, Alex grew up in a home where passion for serving God was a part of everyday life. His mom and dad taught at government schools in Nigeria until Alex was five, and at the same time they devoted themselves to teaching and spreading the Gospel. After coming to the United States for two years to pursue advanced biblical studies, they returned to their native India in 1974, where they founded a Bible school and, later, the New India Evangelistic Association.

Alex's father was a towering figure in Indian evangelism, but he never insisted that either of his sons follow in his professional footsteps. Indeed, first Alex's older brother, then Alex entered medical school. By the time he was twenty-seven, Alex was a rising star in the medical profession.

And then his father was diagnosed with stage IV cancer. Alex watched this man of indomitable faith and strength waste away, while surrounded by his loving family and being cared for by Alex's older brother. After his father's death, as Alex returned to the mission hospital where he was serving a two-year commitment, he felt an undeniable leading from God to go back home and spend three months in prayer.

Not understanding precisely why he was doing so, Alex nevertheless resigned his position at the hospital and went back to South India in obedience to God's prompting. By the end of the three months, Alex knew that his true calling was to carry on his father's evangelistic work.

Alex and his wife, Lali, moved to Bihar, one of the poorest regions in India, to plant churches and establish a Bible school. They soon felt God leading them powerfully toward ministry to children, which resulted in their establishment of fourteen schools that serve some 3,000 students, as well as about the same number of children's homes housing some 480 orphans and destitute children.

They were blessing the lives of thousands of children, but in the meantime their evangelistic efforts, including their church planting, was not going much of anywhere. They were conducting services in Hindi, one of the two official languages of India (along with English). Attendance was reasonably good, but they were just not seeing people come to Christ as readily as they thought should be the case.

In October 2006, Alex met three representatives of The Seed Company, an American Bible Society partner in translation. They were in India to discuss Bible translation needs among indigenous people groups. "What can we do to help you?" they asked.

Alex wasn't sure how to answer their question. He thought, *I live among very poor, illiterate people. Bible translation is for the highly educated, those who know computers . . . Bihar is just the opposite.*

Sensing Alex's hesitancy, one of them rephrased the question: "What is the language spoken here?"

"Again, that didn't make much sense to me," Alex recalled. "We were doing everything in the national language of Hindi. But I told them Angika was the indigenous language."

When the representative typed in the language name, four red stars popped up on the screen.

"Of the language groups remaining without any Scripture, Angika has the highest need," he told Alex.

"Those four red stars had my attention, but still I didn't know what this had to do with me," Alex recalled. "I decided that perhaps I could help The Seed Company and their mission by just bringing pastors together."

Alex was able to use his influence to call a consultation in northern Bihar with a dozen Christian ministries and church-planting agencies to discuss Bible translation there.

"That was a day!" Alex remembered. "After ten years of work in Bihar, I discovered for the first time that there are six spoken languages in the state!"

> "I could see the change that came into these peoples' lives as a result of the stories and Scriptures in their heart languages."

By the end of the meetings, the group had agreed a good first step would be to do an oral Bible storytelling set of twenty-five stories in each of the six languages. Sixty-six percent of the people speaking those languages were illiterate. Nine months later, the stories had been translated by mother-tongue translators whom Alex had helped bring together. These stories were being shared in communities throughout Bihar, both through in-person listening groups and in recorded, audio format.

"The outcome was phenomenal!" Alex said. "I could see the change that came into these peoples' lives as a result of the stories and Scriptures in their heart languages. That made a great impact on my life."

It was just the beginning. Over the next several years, doors of unprecedented opportunity opened up for heart-language Scripture to come to people groups in India with primarily oral language orientation. For the first time, people would know, "God speaks my language."

Alex said that this made all the difference in life transformation for individuals, as well as church attendance. "I could hardly sleep at night!" he said. "God was doing something amazing. In His grace, He put me in touch with His heart for the people of Bihar.

"Today, this is what consumes me. I'm passionate about training, I am passionate about children's work, and I am passionate about medical work. All of that is good. But if you ask me what is driving me—how I spend more than 60 to 70 percent of my day—it is Bible translation.

"Scripture in the heart languages is what is actually opening the kingdom; that is what is blessing the people here in Bihar," Alex said. "We believe God is on a mission of transformation. Unlike men's effort at self-reformation, God's work does not merely tinker with society; it changes it from the inside out. It operates at the heart level."

A God of Surprises

Like Alex walking away from a promising medical career to take up his father's mantle, my life was taking an unexpected turn as I joined the Bible movement. In fact, I suspect that if you made a careful study of the people, throughout the history of our faith, who have done things in God's name, most of them would tell you that when God's call came into their lives, it was very unexpected. I think about the Apostle Paul, knocked off his horse onto the ground by a blinding vision of the risen Christ; David, the youngest son of Jesse,

> "... I suspect that if you made a careful study of the people, throughout the history of our faith, who have done things in God's name, most of them would tell you that when God's call came into their lives, it was very unexpected."

standing in his house with anointing oil running down his forehead as he hears the prophet Samuel announcing that he is to be king of God's people; Mary, the young girl from Nazareth who is visited by an angel and informed that she is to bear the Messiah ... and the list goes on.

The point is that when we sign on to a life committed to God's purposes, we are in for the unexpected. But the good news is that when we place our complete trust in Him, He always goes with us, one way or another. My family and I were about to learn this in an unforgettable way.

Food for Thought

- In order to follow God we have to radically trust, letting everything go.

- God is on a mission of transformation, changing society from the inside out and operating at the heart level.

- When we sign on to a life committed to God's purposes, we are in for a wild ride—but God always brings us safely home.

Questions to Consider

1. Have you ever sensed God asking you to do something you didn't expect? How did you respond? What obstacles did you have to overcome to follow God's invitation?

2. What is the greatest risk in following God's lead in an unexpected direction? What is the greatest risk in not following?

3. Have you ever been so passionate about something you couldn't sleep at night? What was it? If not, what could you be passionate about?

Chapter 8

LEAVING THE AMERICAN DREAM BEHIND

And I said to the man who stood at the gate of the year:
"Give me a light that I may tread safely into the unknown."
And he replied:
"Go out into the darkness and put your
hand into the Hand of God.
That shall be to you better than light
and safer than a known way."

Minnie Louise Haskins

For a time, all Rita and I could see were the obstacles between us and the mission field. I am sure it was because both of us were still relatively new at this whole business of following God wherever He led. It was scary for us, at first, when all we could do was trust God. It took a few years for us to figure out that all we can ever do, anytime, in business or in missions, is trust God.

But right then, all we could see were the challenges we—we, not God—had to solve. We needed to sell the house. We needed to raise our monthly financial support. And we needed to keep a low profile as we made these arrangements, because I didn't want to lose my job before we had secured our financial support.

There were so many hurdles. We had only lived in our home in Florida for three years, so we had little equity built up. The 1980s housing market was down, interest rates were up around 14 percent, and people weren't buying. Thousands and thousands of homes were for sale in the Tampa market. We were told it could take six to nine months or longer to sell a house in those market conditions.

On the other hand, if we listed our home with a Realtor, my company might find out and I could be out of a job. We couldn't go nine months without a paycheck. Selling the house privately and trusting God to bring a buyer seemed like the only solution.

> "It was scary for us, at first, when all we could do was trust God. It took a few years for us to figure out that all we can ever do, anytime, in business or in missions, is trust God."

But we thought God might need a while to locate our buyer. So, Rita went to work making a hand-painted sign on plywood. It had a cute house painted on it and said, "For Sale." It touched my heart—and, I think, God's heart—to see Rita put our home on the market and place the provision for our family into His hands. It showed how fully and deeply committed she was to following God's lead.

One Friday night we said, "Okay, tonight's the night. We'll put the sign out." We prayed over the sign, and then the kids helped install it in our front yard before going to bed. We were giving God nine months to sell the house. We hoped that would be enough time.

The next morning was pancake day at the Peterson house; I loved making pancakes for my family on the weekend. That morning, the griddle was going, the pancakes were hot, and Wes and Jordan were helping me. Corrie was only two. We were all having fun. Ever since the Sunday meltdown years before, I had become more involved in weekend life.

Knock, knock, knock. "Somebody's at the door," someone said. We all ran to answer it. I opened the door to a middle-aged couple. The woman was telling her husband, "Honey, I love it! This is it."

"We'd like to see your home," the man said.

I said, "Sure, come on in."

They bought our house over pancakes! In shock, I explained to them that we'd just put the sign out the night before and thought it would take at least six to nine months to sell, so we weren't prepared to move until summer. I also told them about the Bible translation training in Mexico coming up.

"No problem," the man said. "We'll buy the house now, and you can rent it from us until you leave for training. We don't need it until summer, anyway."

God got it done in twenty-four hours without our even listing the house! It was straight out of Isaiah 65:24: "Even before they finish praying to me, I will answer their prayers" (GNT).

Is Anything Too Hard for the LORD?

Now we faced the hurdle of raising our support. The application asked the question, "Will your local church support you?" I wrote

"No." Our church was a denominational church and I knew their support went to their great global missions efforts. I didn't even want to ask.

The fact was, I didn't want to ask *anybody* for money. I was accustomed to making a good salary, and the thought of "begging" (at least, that was how I thought of it) was pretty tough.

Rita said, "Roy, you can't speak for the church if you haven't even talked to them."

"No, but I know they're not going to support us."

"Well," Rita said, "I think it's wrong to say that without first asking the church." God sided with Rita, as I learned when I read James 4:2: "You do not have what you want because you do not ask God for it" (GNT).

"Okay," I said. "But I don't want to go to Dr. Boehmer. I don't even know how to get in to see the senior pastor in this megachurch."

Then I found out that it wasn't that hard. I called the church office, and the pastor gave me an appointment. Even though it was a large congregation, he knew who Rita and I were, because we were active in the church.

When I met Dr. Boehmer, I learned he had a heart for missions, and it really surprised me to learn that he loved the Wycliffe organization. After discovering we had been accepted, Dr. Boehmer became very interested. In my mind, I said a silent word of thanks to God for my wife's wisdom.

We talked a little more, and Dr. Boehmer asked how much money we needed. He then recommended to the church board that the church contribute 30 percent of our support. Sure enough, for the next fifteen years, they would cover one-third of our support.

I had wanted to avoid humiliation; I didn't want to be turned down. I just wanted to check "no" on the application and be done with it. But as soon as my pride was out of the way, all it took was one God-ordained visit for our support to skyrocket.

After I had learned that lesson it was easier for me to ask the next time. Our church in New York also said yes. Our church in Rhode Island said yes. Our church in Schenectady said yes. Boom, boom, boom—they all said yes, and we had 75 percent of our support. "Is anything too hard for the LORD?" (Genesis 18:14, GNT). Obviously, as I was learning, the answer is "No!"

Taking another step of faith, I sent letters to about forty local churches that I thought might be open to inviting a missionary to speak. A few days later, a little church not far from our home responded.

"We're having a missions weekend. We would like you to speak on Sunday morning," they said.

It was the only church out of forty that answered my letter. On Sunday, Rita and I showed up at the church. They seated us, and before long, they introduced me. I stepped onto the platform, took my place in the pulpit, and scanned the congregation.

That's when I spotted them: David Hensley, senior vice president of Eckerd Drugs, and his wife, Lori, were sitting right there in front of me. They lived in Atlanta. What was the senior VP of my biggest account with American Greetings doing in this tiny church outside of Tampa, out of all of the hundreds of churches in the area—and on the one day I was supposed to get up in front and announce my plans to go to the mission field?

To say I was scared hardly captures my emotions in that moment. In fact, there is no one word for how I felt. Caught, embarrassed, exposed, terrified . . . all of these feelings raced through me as I faced the congregation that Sunday morning.

But there I was, and there they were. The good folks of the church sat in their pews, looking up at me expectantly. What else could I do? I shared my testimony, beginning with my conversion while studying the Bible with two men in a Mexican prison. I talked about how God had blessed me and moved me up the ladder from being a shoe salesman to being an executive with American Greetings. I shared my passion for unreached people groups and our call to be missionaries. I poured out my heart.

That Sunday morning, I faced my deep fear of insecurity. Of course, I realize now that God had orchestrated it all. As soon as the pastor closed the service, I hurried to the door to speak with the Hensleys.

"Great to see you, David and Lori. I'm surprised to see you here."

David explained that they had come to Tampa on business and decided to stay over for Sunday worship.

"David, I have no idea how God is going to work everything out. It's a walk of faith," I said. "I'm really struggling with when to make this public and how AGC will take it when I do."

He shook my hand and looked me in the eye. "Roy, you can trust us with this." That's all he said, and he kept his promise. A few months later, David and Lori said they wanted to help support us financially on the field. Now retired and twenty-six years later, they continue to support us prayerfully.

Facing my fears seemed to be my portion for this season of life. In those days, I often thought of the time when Peter stepped out of the boat. When he started to sink, Jesus took his hand and lifted him up (Matthew 14:31). In our case, God hadn't exactly told Rita and me to step out of the boat that Sunday in Tampa; He actually gave us a gentle push. *Trust Me, Roy,* He said. *Stop hiding, and trust Me. This is a risky adventure, and you can't play it safe.*

Letting Go, Letting God

I knew that the time was fast approaching when I would need to speak to my boss, Richard, about what I was planning to do. The house was sold, our support was pledged, and I knew that I had to stop putting off what I was afraid would be a very difficult conversation.

After all, Richard had been so good to me. I had worked hard for American Greetings, and he had supported me all the way. He had trained me and done everything in his power to help me succeed. Besides all that, he had become a friend. And now I would be telling him that I was resigning. I was not looking forward to it.

But I made an appointment with him and he flew into Tampa to meet with me. When I walked in that day, he was holding a letter—an offer from the company for a promotion. AGC's business was booming, and they needed to make some rapid promotions of those whom they considered to be their best people; I was one of those they had chosen.

But money and position no longer meant anything to me. My passions lay in other directions now. "Richard, I am deeply honored by this offer," I said, "but I can't accept it. In fact, I came here to offer my resignation." I told him about our mission plans.

"Is this a done deal or will you reconsider?" Richard asked. He held out the promotion letter. "You've earned this,"

I shook my head. "I'm honored, but I can't. I've made a commitment."

With reluctance, my friend and colleague accepted my resignation. When he did, a weight lifted from my mind and heart. I'd faced my greatest fear! I'd taken a leap of faith and turned loose of the financial security I'd spent nearly fifteen years building. God had confirmed that this crucial step was one we had to take. Our total dependence was on Him, and He had proven Himself time and time again.

> "God had confirmed that this crucial step was one we had to take.
> Our total dependence was on Him, and He had proven Himself time and time again."

I wish that I could say that was the watershed moment when I released all my doubts and insecurities and placed my complete trust in God. However, that wasn't the case; I still had more to learn about giving God free rein in my life.

During training in North Carolina, while Rita and the four kids were having a wonderful time, I was desperately struggling. God had drawn our imaginations into the mission of reaching Bible-less people groups through Bible translation, and they had chosen me to work in government relations in Ecuador.

With no background or training in this area, I doubted my ability to do this job. As a result, I was feeling keenly the pressure of the decision to uproot Rita and the kids, to leave their great schools and everything familiar, and to move halfway around the world. It was keeping me awake at night.

Dean, Wes, Jordan and Corrie in Florida, 1985

Dean in 10th grade

Roy, Rita, Wes, Jordan and Corrie
in Quito, Ecuador

Government Relations Meeting
in Roy & Rita's home. Quito, Ecuador

Bible translation team, Colorado People, Congama, Ecuador

Worship with Mincaye of the
Waorani people, At Wycliffe
Headquarters, Orlando

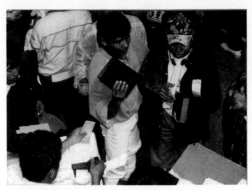

Bible Dedication Celebration in Guatemala

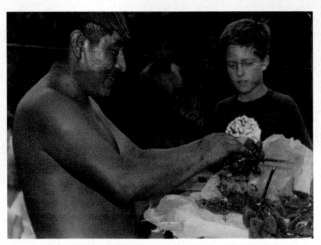

Wes watching on as the achiote is being broken open
for the dyeing process of his hair. The Colorados loved
that our boys wanted to look like them.

Wes and Jordan visiting Colorado people, Congona,
Ecuador

Prayers and tears of joy, His Word has arrived

Roy with Elias and his brother from the Secoya people
of the Amazon in Roy's home.

Wes and Corrie
with a jungle umbrella

Roy & Rita having just landed in the Amazon

Making our way to Bible dedication
celebration with painted faces

Rita filming the Colorados in the jungle per their request
to record history for future generations.

Ecuadorian President Rodrigo Borja Cevallos asks Dave Underwood (Ecuador SIL director) how to pronounce Waorani words, as Roy Peterson and Dave Farah listen in. Quito, 1992

Roy Meeting with Chuck Colson in Quito, Ecuador

Bible Dedication parade in Santiago Atitlan, Guatemala

Choir at Bible Dedication Celebration in Guatemala

Bible Dedication, Santiago Atitlan, Guatemala

Roy and Rita with Pedro & Anna from Tzutujil people
of Mayan decent in Guatemala

Leaving Guatemala for Wycliffe role
as President in California, 1997

Roy & Rita with Waorani believers who've chosen to "follow
Jesus's trail", with Steve Saint, Amsterdam, 2000.

Groundbreaking for Wycliffe Headquarters, Orlando, FL, 2001

International Relations at Lausanne
2010, South Africa

Garden Tomb, Jerusalem, 2011

Meeting with Nigerian translators
and Dr. Katy Barnwell

Teaching a Bible study
on Mount Arbel, Israel, 2012

ABS Board praying over Roy and Rita after being
elected as the 28th president of American Bible Society

Roy & Rita Peterson – Installation as President to American Bible
Society, Holy Trinity Lutheran Church, New York City, June 2014

Roy and Rita with children impacted by war working on
Trauma Healing workbook, DRC, Africa, August 2016

Roy & Rita greeting Pope Francis at the The Blessing
of Long Life: Elderly and Grandparents Encounter,
Vatican, Rome, September 2014

Roy greeting His Holiness Pope Tawadros II,
118th Pope of Alexandria and Patriarch of the
See of St. Mark Egypt, December 2014.

Roy and Rita, with ABS Chairman, Nick & Tina Athens,
Mario Paredes, Archbishop Paglia and Pope Francis at
the World Meeting of Families gathering, Philadelphia,
PA, September 2015.

Roy and Rita – National Prayer Breakfast, Washington, D.C., February 2016

Roy and Rita with radio station celebrating Trauma Healing Ministry, DRC, Africa, August 2016

Roy and Rita with the 2016 Board of Trustees at the American Bible Society Bicentennial Gala

Roy & Rita at the American Bible Society Bicentennial Gala, May 2016

Roy addressing Staff and Guests at the American Bible Society Bicentennial Gala, May 2016

My heart tugged in one direction, while deep insecurity pulled hard the other way. *What am I doing? I know nothing about linguistics and Bible translation—and I'm supposed to represent this ministry to the government officials?* It seemed absurd. I didn't even speak Spanish and we were going to a South American country!

One day, during my routine devotions, I was reading in Proverbs when God spoke directly to my heart from His Word. "Show me someone who does a good job, and I will show you someone who is better than most and worthy of the company of kings" (Proverbs 22:29, GNT).

I stared at and read that verse over and over. God was preparing me for something. I sensed Him speaking to my heart: *Roy, I will go with you before government leaders. Just as I was with you before business leaders, I will go with you in this work.*

> "We have kept the image of God going before us as the assurance for every step of our journey in ministry and in life. We have resolved to allow God to lead in whatever direction He chooses, and we will do our best to follow faithfully."

That day, I drove a spiritual stake in the ground. The word of God in Proverbs spoke powerfully and personally to me. It was a holy moment for me. I felt it too deeply to tell anyone—except Rita; I couldn't wait to tell her!

We have kept the image of God going before us as the assurance for every step of our journey in ministry and in life. We have resolved to allow God to lead in whatever direction He chooses, and we will do our best to follow faithfully.

The Gideon Strategy

As Rita and I were fast learning, it is not up to us to understand everything about God's call; it is only up to us to follow. I am often reminded, especially since my career has focused on getting Bibles to as many people around the world as possible, of the namesake of another Bible organization, Gideons International. It is said that when they gathered for their initial organizational meeting, they engaged in a time of prayer focused on what they would be called. At the end of that prayer time, William J. Knights, one of the founders, said to the gathering, "We shall be called Gideons."[1]

> "... it is not up to us to understand everything about God's call; it is only up to us to follow."

Why Gideons? There is hardly a more unlikely hero in all of the Bible than Gideon. When the angel of the Lord came to call him to lead God's people against the oppressions of the Midianites, Gideon was hiding in a winepress, trying to conceal the wheat he was threshing from the bad guys.

The first words out of the angel's mouth were, "The LORD is with you, brave and mighty man!" (Judges 6:12, GNT). What happened next is almost comical. You can almost see Gideon looking around to see whom the angel is actually talking to. When he figures out that he is the one being addressed, he goes into a litany of all the reasons

1. Gideons International, "Our History"; http://www.gideons.org/AboutUs/OurHistory.aspx (accessed June 12, 2016).

he isn't so sure that God is being completely straight with him. It is almost as if he were saying, "Excuse me? I'm looking around here, and I'm not seeing a lot of evidence of God's presence."

The heavenly messenger then said, "Go with all your great strength and rescue Israel from the Midianites. I myself am sending you" (Judges 6:14, GNT).

Once again, Gideon said, in effect, "Um, excuse me? I think you have me confused with someone else; my clan is not exactly a powerhouse, and I'm only the kid brother, at that. Maybe you were thinking of somebody in one of those big southern tribes?"

God continued to assure Gideon that he is the chosen one, and he proceeded—very graciously, in my opinion—to submit to several tests, until Gideon was finally convinced that God is really involved in the situation.

In the following passages of Judges 6, we read how Gideon conducted his campaign against the Midianites, who were vastly superior in numbers and in military wherewithal. First, at God's bidding, he trimmed his fighting force from 32,000 down to 10,000, by excusing all those who were afraid. I'm actually kind of surprised that he had 10,000 left after that. Next, he eliminated those of the 10,000 who drank their water the wrong way, again at God's command. At the end, he was left with 300 soldiers to go up against a Midianite army that numbered in the thousands; the Bible says that they were "like a swarm of locusts; and they had as many camels as there are grains of sand on the seashore" (Judges 7:12, GNT).

According to the plan, Gideon divided his men into three groups and passed out ram's horn bugles and clay pots with lamps inside. Waiting until the middle of the night, they blew their trumpets and dashed their pots to the ground, allowing the lamps inside to flare up into flame. They shouted, "For the LORD and for Gideon!" (v. 18).

What happened next could hardly have been more amazing and unexpected. Instead of grabbing their spears and easily annihilating the tiny Israelite force, the Midianites were thrown in a complete panic. They rushed back and forth—many of them barely awake—and started killing each other in their confusion. Soon they were in a full, panicked retreat, and Gideon's army took the victory almost as easily as walking down Main Street.

> "We did not understand how we were going to overcome the many obstacles facing us at the beginning of our journey. But one by one, we saw those obstacles fall as God proved faithful, over and over again."

No wonder that the men gathered for prayer in 1899 at the Janesville, Wisconsin, YMCA chose the name "Gideon" for their fledgling group. Like Gideon of old, they knew they faced great darkness and many opponents with only the small lights they bore with them. Like Gideon's army, they were few. But also like Gideon, they believed they were being called by God to the work of spreading the Good News by getting Bibles into as many places as possible.

In so many ways, the call Rita and I felt was similar. We did not understand how we were going to overcome the many obstacles facing us at the beginning of our journey. But one by one, we saw those obstacles fall as God proved faithful, over and over again.

Food for Thought

- While stepping out to follow God can be scary, all we can do is trust God.

- When we are following God in faith, we can be assured that He is stronger than any problem, complication, or barrier.

- It is not up to us to understand everything about God's call; it is only up to us to follow.

Questions to Consider

1. Have you, or someone you know, taken a course of action that seemed to make little sense, solely because of the belief that God was calling for it? What happened? How did it impact them—or others?

2. If you knew you could not fail, what would you attempt? How might God be calling you to take a step of faith, despite your fears?

3. Is it difficult to trust God with your finances? What changes would you have to make to fully let go of this area?

Chapter 9

NEW LANGUAGE, NEW CULTURE

---

*A ship in a harbor is safe, but that is
not what ships are built for.*

John A. Shedd

We sat in the line of vehicles at the checkpoint, and I was
really nervous. You can understand why. It was January
1988; fifteen years earlier I had crossed this border and ended up
in prison.

I could feel my pulse starting to accelerate as it all came back.
I was especially anxious when I remembered how the guards at
the prison had made me sign papers I didn't understand as a
condition of my release, requiring me to report to the Mexican
authorities each month. Of course, once I had crossed the border
back into the United States on that long-ago day, I would have
taken a solemn oath that I would never cross the border for the
rest of my life.

And yet, here we were, and now the border guard was asking for
my passport and those of my family. As he walked away to check
our information against the Mexican border control system, I kept
telling myself that the vetting process had turned up no evidence
that I was ever in Mexico to begin with. And I prayed furiously.

The border guard walked back, handed us our documents, smiled, and waved us through. I started breathing again.

We were on our way to the Americas Field Training course, a part of our orientation onboarding process. We were slated for a position in Quito, Ecuador, and our experiences in Mexico were designed to immerse us in Latin American language, customs, and culture. We would be living with a Mexican family, eating with them, worshipping with them, learning their language, and adapting to completely different customs, societal expectations, and ways of doing things.

We learned, for example, that in this culture, the men of the house were expected to eat first, and the women shared whatever was left. When I realized that Rita and our three-year-old daughter Corrie were not getting much to eat, I started cutting back.

We learned that using an outdoor shower isn't so bad, as long as you heat up a bucket of water beforehand.

We learned that "running around like a chicken with its head cut off" is not just a colloquial expression. I'll never forget the look on Rita's face when she decapitated a chicken she was about to prepare for our meal and it jumped out of the pan and ran around the yard for a minute before realizing it was dead.

Speaking of Rita's experiences in the kitchen, we learned that you really can make a pizza over an open fire. I guarantee you that once Rita mastered this particular culinary art form, we forgot all about Pizza Hut.

She also learned that you can wash clothes by hand in an outdoor washtub and run them through a hand wringer—another real-life demonstration of what we had previously experienced only as a metaphor. Our clothes had never been cleaner.

I visited with men in our community and built relationships even as I was overcoming the language barrier. Dean often joined me when we traveled to small villages in the area to share our faith with others. Wes and Jordan worked diligently on home schooling to keep up with their classes back in the US.

In other words, when we look back on our time spent in Mexico, it comes down to the word our daughter, Corrie, who was three years old at the time, used to describe the experience: "Excitement!" It was a time of exponential growth, not only in our Spanish language skills and cultural sensitivity, but also in our faith and our willingness to allow God to guide each day of our lives.

That's not to say we didn't have some obstacles to overcome. While we felt reasonably prepared for the differences we encountered in many areas, we weren't really prepared for the level of isolation we felt when no one spoke our language. I particularly remember when, during a youth meeting, someone surprisingly played a song in English. We were completely caught off-guard by the way we hung onto every word.

And then we remembered: this was what Bible translation was all about. This experience served to remind us that we were preparing ourselves to go to Ecuador to help make it possible for the Quechua people and others to hang onto every word of the Bible as they heard and read it in their mother tongue.

Overcoming Limitations

As I think about how valuable it was for us to live in a country with a different language and different customs, I'm reminded of a famous quote from Mark Twain: "Travel is fatal to prejudice, bigotry, and narrow-mindedness, and many of our people need it sorely on these accounts. Broad, wholesome, charitable views of men and things cannot be acquired by vegetating in one little corner of the earth all one's lifetime."[1] I could not agree more. It's so easy to have a very narrow and restricted view of other peoples and cultures, simply because they live their entire lives in a place where they constitute the majority. After all, if everyone you know looks like you, speaks like you, thinks like you, and lives pretty much the same way you do, naturally you're going to view with suspicion anyone who is "different." If I could prescribe one single thing for people that would make us better citizens of the world and more inclusive, compassionate, and flexible in our thinking, that would be to travel abroad and experience different languages and cultures.

> "'Travel is fatal to prejudice, bigotry, and narrow-mindedness, and many of our people need it sorely on these accounts. Broad, wholesome, charitable views of men and things cannot be acquired by vegetating in one little corner of the earth all one's lifetime.'"
>
> (Mark Twain)

But beyond the cultural and linguistic experiences that deepened us socially, our time in Mexico was also pivotal in deepening

---

1. Mark Twain, *Innocents Abroad/Roughing It* (original publication Hartford, CT: American Publishing Co., 1869); available at Project Gutenberg (online), http://www.gutenberg.org/files/3176/3176-h/3176-h.htm (accessed June 22, 2016).

NEW LANGUAGE, NEW CULTURE

both our trust in God's leading and the conviction that we were walking the path He had chosen for us. We had a profound sense that we were in Mexico in direct response to His Word, preparing ourselves to take that same Word to a hurting and hungry world. We began to experience what happens to obstacles that we might think insurmountable, once we simply proceed in faith as God leads.

There is a quote in Shane Claiborne's book *The Irresistible Revolution* that speaks to me: "We have insulated ourselves from miracles. We no longer live with such reckless faith that we need them."[2] As my family and I faced our own limitations—social, economic, linguistic, and cultural—with an inadequate confidence that God would make a way for His will to be done, we began to see our limitations replaced, time after time, by God's gracious provision. In fact, in a way, each limitation was transformed into one more opportunity for God to demonstrate His limitless capability.

I was reminded continually of Paul's words in 2 Corinthians 12:9, where he relates God's response to the "thorn in the flesh" that the great apostle longed to be delivered from: "'My grace is all you need, for my power is greatest when you are weak.' I am most happy, then, to be proud of my weaknesses, in order to feel the protection of Christ's power over me" (GNT). Paul is describing almost exactly what we were learning: God is not only unlimited by our limitations; He actually uses them to magnify His amazing power in our lives!

2. Shane Claiborne, *The Irresistible Revolution: Living as an Ordinary Radical*, Updated and Expanded edition (Grand Rapids: Zondervan, 2016), 24.

Fearless Faith

When we are willing to step out in faith, there is no place on earth that God cannot reach. A few years ago, Rita and I saw this demonstrated in dramatic fashion when we went to Nepal.

The rugged peaks of the Himalayas form most of the terrain of this remote Asian country; frequently, those living in one of the small villages in the isolated mountain valleys are not even aware that another village exists on the other side of the same mountain. And not only is the terrain difficult; Nepal has in recent years become a major location for human trafficking, as unscrupulous people prey on the fears and aspirations of young Nepalese women and sell them into sex slavery in India and other places.

> "When we are willing to step out in faith, there is no place on earth that God cannot reach."

In the midst of such difficult circumstances, however, God is using the faithful efforts of Nepalese Christians to take the good news of hope and salvation into the almost-inaccessible mountain villages of the Himalayas. Rita and I met a group of young men on what is called a "rapid assessment team," or, as they laughingly call themselves, "RATs."

These brave young men leave their homes for weeks at a time to travel on foot up into the mountains. Taking nothing but what they can carry in their backpacks, they use GPS devices to document the locations of the villages they encounter—most of these places are not found on any current maps—and they assess the languages of the people they meet.

They go out, not knowing where they will stop or what they will eat, since they are traveling into areas where the location and density of human habitation is unknown. When they return, they provide real-time intelligence about Bible translation needs in the places they have mapped, along with information that will aid the next wave of evangelists and translators.

I had the opportunity to learn the story of one of these faithful, fearless "RATs"; we'll call him Geet. His father, whom we'll refer to as Sanjay, came to know Christ as a result of working as a porter and guide for groups going on mountain treks in his native region.

Sanjay noticed that the people in a particular church group from Singapore were different from many of those he worked for: they were kinder, more interested in him as a person. They sometimes asked to carry their own bags, and they even pitched in with the work in the camp at night.

The group leader often called Sanjay aside to spend time with him, talking about Jesus. Eventually, Sanjay claimed Christ as his Savior: the first in his ethnic group to do so. Before long, Sanjay felt God leading him to translate the Bible into his native language so that others could hear and understand the Good News. With the help of a missionary, he translated the entire Bible: an astounding accomplishment for anyone.

Today, Sanjay leads a national translation organization for Nepal, and there are now thousands of believers and many churches in his native region. He and his wife have raised Geet and mentored other young Nepalese Christians to carry on the work of taking the Bible to the isolated hamlets of the mountain valleys. When Geet leaves home for one of his weeks-long assessment treks as a RAT, he knows that the prayers of his faithful father and mother are accompanying him.

Thanks to the faith of people like Sanjay, his wife, and his son, Geet, God's Word is going into some of the most remote and difficult places on earth. However, these fearless servants need our help. They need for us to cover them in prayer, and they need those of us with financial resources to provide the assistance they require to respond to the needs of the Nepalese people who are still without the Bible.

> ". . . God's Word is going into some of the most remote and difficult places on earth. However, these fearless servants need our help. They need for us to cover them in prayer, and they need those of us with financial resources to provide the assistance they require to respond to the needs of [all] people who are still without the Bible."

Sanjay, Geet, and their brothers and sisters in Christ have proven, over and over again, their willingness to be the hands and feet of Jesus in the steep mountain passes and hidden valleys of Nepal. But they need people like you and me to be their partners in this vital kingdom work.

Food for Thought

- God often uses our limitations and weaknesses as opportunities for His glory.

- When we are willing to step out in faith, there is no place on earth that God cannot reach.

- God's Word is going into some of the most remote places on earth, but these faithful servants need our help in furthering the work.

Questions to Consider

1. What experiences have you had with other cultures—at home or abroad? How have these experiences expanded your view of the world, others, or yourself?

2. What comforts do you currently enjoy? Do these comforts ever prevent you from taking risks? Are they worth holding onto?

3. Have you ever experienced a miracle, or do you know someone who has? What changed after this event?

Chapter 10

THROUGH THE DARK VALLEY

Hear me! Save me now!
Be my refuge to protect me;
My defense to save me.

Psalm 31:2 (GNT)

Toward the end of our time in Mexico, as we were looking forward to beginning the transition to our first actual assignment in Ecuador, Dean asked to speak with Rita. When he looked at her with his brow furrowed, something grabbed Rita's heart. She knew it was serious.

"I know what I'm supposed to do," he told her. "The Lord wants me to stay in the States and finish twelfth grade. I believe He wants me to live with my father during my senior year." At that time we weren't sure that Sal, Dean's biological father, had a personal relationship with Christ. "I want to be a witness to him and lead him to the Lord," Dean explained to his mom.

But we were bound for Ecuador as a family! We had already registered Dean at Alliance Academy in Quito. We had his passport and visa. For us to leave Dean in Dallas when we were moving to Equador was heartbreaking for us to contemplate.

"I'll be in twelfth grade, and then I'll be at college," he explained. "This is the one chance that I've got to influence him. I want to be sure he'll be in heaven with me someday"

"Are you sure?" Rita asked. "We'll pray with you for guidance."

Dean cut his mother off. "I know this is God's will for me."

That night, when Rita and I were alone, we held each other and wept. We didn't want to be separated from our son. I felt that Dean was as much my child as the other three were, and he knew it. When I looked at our handsome, sixteen-year-old son, I still saw the two-year-old I had met when I first started dating Rita and the curly haired four-year-old ring bearer who had walked down the aisle at our wedding. Now I was taking this decision personally and it seemed like I was losing him; I didn't want that. It felt like a deep wound was being inflicted on me—not to mention what it was doing to Rita.

> "What could we do? What should we do? We had taught our children to love God, to listen to the Holy Spirit's leading, and to make decisions based on the Word."

Not knowing a lot about Sal's values, we were worried. I regret to admit that unlike Dean, who cried as he prayed for his father, neither Rita nor I were praying so earnestly for Sal to put his trust in Jesus. Dean's well-being was our only concern.

What could we do? What should we do? We had taught our children to love God, to listen to the Holy Spirit's leading, and to make decisions based on the Word. Dean seemed to be doing that. At age sixteen, he was demonstrating a great level of discipleship.

We hadn't been able to change his mind; he would spend his senior year with Sal and his family.

In a month, we left Mexico to return to the US and pack our belongings to move to Quito, Ecuador. We were eager to begin helping the tribal people of the Amazon Basin and Andes Mountains receive God's Word for the first time. But when the time came for Dean's father to pick him up, a heavy curtain of sadness descended. We held back the flood of tears until the car began to back away.

Getting to Work in Ecuador

When we arrived in Ecuador in the summer of 1988, Bible translation work was underway with eight different indigenous people groups. We were in a prayer support group for the Colorado Indians. The first translators had arrived in this region in the 1950s to serve the smaller people groups of the Amazon River Basin, so by the time Rita and I arrived, much translation work had been done. New Testaments were being completed and distributed in the heart languages of the Secoya, the Cofán, the Colorado, and the Huaorani (also known as the Waorani or Waodani). In the 1950s, the Huaorani had killed five missionaries, so it was especially meaningful to attend worship celebrations with them and witness the ways that God was bringing beauty from the ashes of the past.

We were also making plenty of adjustments to a new country and a new culture, not to mention that we had just relocated from the Florida Gulf coast to Quito, which is situated 10,000 feet above sea level. Watching God at work among the people of the Amazon region was breathtaking—and so was walking from my house to the office.

During our years in Ecuador, the Colorado people came to hold a special place in our hearts, and they still do. In Spanish, the word *colorado* means red, and the tribe's name comes from their practice of dyeing their hair red. They break open *achiote* plants, crush the bright red seeds, mix the powder with Vaseline-like oil, and then coat their hair. They look like they are wearing red umbrellas, and as a matter of fact, when it rains, the drops hit their hair and roll right off. During one trip, Wes and Jordan had their hair painted this way. The kids loved walking around with giant leaves to protect their heads in the rainforest.

The dedication of the Colorado New Testament was one of our lifetime highlights. It was an amazing ceremony. Ecuadorian tribes, dignitaries, and guests traveled from near and far to attend the celebration. The Quechua from the highlands came; the Huaorani traveled from their jungle villages. The Secoya and the Cofán came. The event was like the "united nations of Ecuador." The worship felt like heaven.

Our days were full, and the months flew by. Soon our first Christmas in Ecuador was upon us. Dean was coming to visit us for the holidays, and we couldn't wait. On December 21, Rita and I were like kids eager to open gifts as we stood at the gate hand in hand, searching avidly for Dean and Rita's parents among the deplaning passengers. Finally, we spotted them on the tarmac.

We hugged Rita's folks, and we grabbed Dean tight. "We're a complete family again," I said. Though Dean was just as glad to see us, I also sensed a sorrow in him as I hugged him a second time. Later I would learn why.

When we got home, Corrie, Wes, and Jordan demanded all of Dean's attention. They had a lot of catching up to do. The kids told him about their jungle trips, red hair, and new friends. And they showed off their Spanish-speaking abilities. Dean talked a bit about driving and a little about school. Rita prepared dinner. Just watching my family, hearing the kids laugh and tell animated stories, was such a joy.

Second Thoughts

After the dishes were done and the kids and their grandparents were in bed, Rita and I finally had time to sit and talk with Dean.

"I made a mistake," Dean blurted out. "I shouldn't have moved in with my father. He doesn't seem to understand my faith or want to listen. He won't support me going to church. He makes fun of my Christian music."

We were alarmed. Our hearts broke as we listened quietly, trying to decide what to say. We knew how much he loved his father and how hard this must be for him.

"He's moving again," Dean added, explaining that Sal had taken a job in Houston. Dean paused before he said, "I really want to move here with you."

We were immediately thrilled by this possibility. Yet we quickly began to think about some of the complications this would involve. We began talking about them: it was Christmas vacation time and the schools were closed; there was no one in the mission office to start processing paperwork for Dean to stay; we would need to renew his visa. . . .

"I want to stay here," he repeated.

"And we want you here!" we told him. But we knew several other things would have to be addressed: school officials in Quito would have to agree to the transfer; we wondered if the high school curriculum here was in sync with Texas schools; Dean was college-bound, which meant he would be with us for only five months before he would leave again.

He had already applied to some good colleges. "Will moving adversely affect any of that?" I asked. None of us knew the answer, but we assumed it could.

Dean quietly listened as I summarized the conclusions we'd drawn. "It's nearly January now, and you'll graduate in May. Your grades are good, and you've already applied to several Christian colleges. You'll get accepted by a good university, and you'll be off to college in just a few more months." (Dean planned to work and play his trumpet at a Christian family camp when summer came.) "You can make it five more months, can't you?" I asked.

Though Dean agreed to go back to graduate and prepare for college, he was hesitant. We sensed he was really struggling. He didn't have any friends in his new high school, he said.

Our hearts were heavy at the end of the vacation as we put Dean back on a plane for Texas. After he arrived in Dallas, Sal moved his family to Houston, and Dean started at his third school in less than a year.

The Call No One Wants to Get

Six weeks later, the phone startled us awake at 3:00 a.m., Sunday morning, February 19, 1989. I picked up the phone and I soon realized it was the call that every parent prays they will never get. It was about Dean. I heard Rita pick up on the extension.

"Dean was in a car accident . . . you need to come now," Sal was saying. He was sobbing so hard that I could barely understand him. "Dean might not live," he said.

That I heard.

I felt numb. As we hung up, Rita grabbed me. "We have to ask people to pray," she said. "Dean's life depends on it." We started calling.

We couldn't get a dial tone for international calls. I finally reached my sister Karen in New York. Within hours, she had marshaled an army of prayer warriors. Later we would learn that literally thousands of people were praying for Dean.

As we understood the events leading up to the accident, Sal had encouraged Dean to meet neighborhood kids and make friends. Because Dean's convictions for the Lord were not shared by many teens, he didn't have many friends. When some boys invited him to a party that night, Dean said no. Sal later confided that he had insisted that Dean go.

Someone at the party had just received a new Mustang. This car had a powerful, 5.0-liter engine and they were all taking turns behind the wheel. What teenager could resist? I know I wouldn't have passed up the opportunity at that age.

Dean, however, was such a good kid. When asked if he wanted a turn at the wheel, he just jumped in the back seat. Apparently, the new, unexperienced driver popped the clutch at such a high rate of speed that the car was airborne for a few seconds before it hit pavement again. The driver lost control, and the car careened into a tree. The two boys sitting in the front seats opened their doors and walked away.

Dean did not.

The decision for me to stay in Ecuador with the other children was made quickly. Somehow, we got Rita onto a flight to Miami, after we had managed to pull together the necessary paperwork for her to leave the country on such short notice. Friends from the mission and the local church helped us every step of the way and also kept up a constant vigil of prayer for our family and for Dean. Rita made it to Houston where Sal picked her up and they went to the hospital where Dean was in the ICU.

She looked around trauma ICU and couldn't see Dean. She had to ask, "which one is he?" The sight of Dean in that bed, unconscious, with tubes and leads running into and all over his swollen body, was almost more than Rita could handle. Later, when she called me from the hospital, she would tell me that when she talked to Dean, his eyelids flickered. It was a wisp of a hope, but we clung to it with all our might.

Rita stayed with Sal and his wife and children, but they spent every available moment at the hospital. Dean would be happy to see the healing that his trauma was bringing to his parents' relationships. They watched, drowning in fear and grief, as Dean's condition deteriorated. At one point, the doctors had to reopen a wound because they feared renewed internal bleeding. He also had a brain bleed that required emergency surgery and the removal of a golf ball–sized piece of his brain.

And still we all prayed, hoped, and refused to believe that God would fail to pull Dean through. Rita continued to sing in her soul a popular song at the time, "Ah, Lord God" by Don Moen. "Nothing, nothing, absolutely nothing, nothing is difficult for thee."

Despite all that, though, Dean was pronounced dead on February 24, 1989, just less than a week after Rita reached his bedside. I learned this just after I landed in Houston with Wes, our second-oldest; Dean had died about an hour before our arrival. I will forever regret not bringing Jordan and Corrie back to the United States too. My heart broke into a thousand pieces. Rita's broke into a million.

As we headed for the hospital, Wes and I cried together. When we arrived, we ran inside to find Rita. Wes grabbed his mother, and so did I. As the three of us stood huddled together in the hospital corridor, a transplant team brushed past us with a cooler marked "Heart Transplant."

"That is Dean's heart," Rita choked out.

Dean's heart—his good, strong heart—would save the life of a Houston man in his fifties who had been on the transplant list.

Two blind people would now see, because of Dean's corneas.

Thirty children with bone cancer would live longer because of Dean's bone marrow.

Burn victims in a children's ward in Galveston, Texas, would have a chance to heal, thanks to his skin.

And Sal, Dean's biological father, along with other loved ones in Dean's extended family, grew in their relationship with Christ during this time. So Dean's fervent prayers were answered—but not the way we had hoped.

At the time, all of this was little consolation to us. Dean's organs would help others heal, but how would *we* heal? We just didn't know how to live without him.

"God," I said silently, "we've given You everything, and now You take our son? Leaving our family, friends, home, and job weren't enough for You? What kind of God are You?" I was so hurt, so angry. In my mind, God had let us down.

But I had let us down, too. Guilt rushed in on top of the grief with such ferocity that I could hardly breathe. Not only had I supported Dean going to Sal's, I was the one who had hauled out all the logical reasons why he should stay with Sal until he graduated.

I want to come live in Ecuador with you . . . I made a mistake . . . Dean's words echoed in my mind. To this day, those words pierce my heart. If he had remained in Ecuador . . . And Sal was thinking, *If only I didn't insist on Dean going out. . .* Pangs of quiet anguish were overtaking us all.

> "The prayers of others carried us, because we were too numb and crushed to be able to pray ourselves."

Our family stumbled through the next weeks and months. The prayers of others carried us, because we were too numb and crushed to be able to pray ourselves.

After the funeral, Rita wrote a letter to our partners and friends. In part it said:

The mighty hand of God was at work during the week Dean was in the hospital, the day he died, and throughout the memorial services held for him in Dallas, Texas; Albany, New York; and Brandon, Florida. . . . While we were waiting for a miracle in Dean's life, we saw, instead, many in his death. . . .

The network of prayer was a beautiful working of God's love. Your calls, cards, gifts and unique gestures of love were a demonstration of Christian love that was not only for us, but for others who watched in awe.... All our expenses have been met through your unexpected and overwhelming generosity. We couldn't think about financial needs at that time, and the Lord provided all we needed through you....

We are grateful, thankful, and hopeful. We have walked through the valley of the shadow of death, but He has walked with us. We have held the hand of sorrow, but our God has made it sweet. We love Him so, and even in our hurt, we feel His love and comfort.

> "It felt as though the earth had shifted all around us. Like Peter after the arrest of Jesus, our souls were sifted like wheat. We felt battered and bruised, and our understanding of God was shaken."

That's what Rita wrote. But that's only in part what I felt. There seemed to be no room in my faith for something as devastating as this. It would take many years and massive amounts of prayer and time in God's Word for me to trudge through the mire of hurt and guilt.

It felt as though the earth had shifted all around us. Like Peter after the arrest of Jesus, our souls were sifted like wheat. We felt battered and bruised, and our understanding of God was shaken. We came very close to quitting everything, walking away. In our deep grief, everything we believed or thought we believed came into question.

Rita's journey to healing was even more agonizing than my own. Work kept me busy and occupied. Rita, however, sank into such despair that at one point, suicidal thoughts bombarded her mind.

After watching her suffer for months and months, I mustered the courage to ask her, "Do you want to move back to the States?" At that point, I was willing to give up everything we hoped to accomplish on the mission field. I cannot possibly explain how difficult it was for me to even put this into words—calling into question everything Rita and I had hoped for up until now, all the plans we had made in faith. We were so crushed and felt so defeated. It felt as if part of us had died along with Dean.

> ". . . God's faithfulness and the prayers of the Christian brothers and sisters who loved us held us up and made it possible for us to take the next breath, the next step."

"What difference would that make?" Rita said. "Dean would still be gone."

She was right, of course. So we pressed on. It wasn't until Rita began seeing a counselor that she began to see the light of day. It took two years. But dealing with our son's death became a defining event in Rita's life, our marriage, and our family. Without seeking to do so, time and again she found herself in a position to help others walk through the valley of the shadow of death. People started coming to her for help, just as Paul mentioned: "He helps us in all our troubles, so that we are able to help others who have all kinds of troubles, using the same help that we ourselves have received from God" (2 Corinthians 1:4, GNT).

Subsequently, Rita went back to school to get her degree in counseling. Today she is a licensed professional counselor and licensed marriage and family therapist. She is writing a book about her own long journey toward healing that will one day help other families heal. She is also trained in trauma healing and grief therapy.

Words of Healing

As I look back, I know that Rita and I could not have survived the unimaginable pain and loss of Dean's death without God's Word in our lives and hearts, and without God's people surrounding us. Even on those days when we woke up wishing that we hadn't, God's faithfulness and the prayers of the Christian brothers and sisters who loved us held us up and made it possible for us to take the next breath, the next step.

> "Through the years I have witnessed God's healing Word provide, not only comfort, but moment-to-moment survival for people like us, those suffering desperate trauma."

Through the years I have witnessed God's healing Word provide, not only comfort, but moment-to-moment survival for people like us, those suffering desperate trauma. I think of Baraka, a woman we met in Rwanda, who has turned deep tragedy into powerful ministry.

A pastor's daughter, Baraka grew up with a heart full of Christian compassion, and she dreamed of being a nurse. But her faith was soon tested. When she was still a teenager, her family was forced to flee the horrendous violence of the Rwandan genocide. Leaving everything behind, they made their way to Congo. Along the road, Baraka saw dead bodies, blood everywhere. Among the refugees in Congo, conditions were difficult and still dangerous, and this young woman saw the ravages of disease all around her.

But God used these hard experiences to sharpen her. Baraka managed to become a nurse in the following years, eventually returning to her homeland when the conflict eased. Yet she soon recognized that her patients' problems were more than just physical. Many were suffering from post-genocide trauma. To fully treat these people, she needed training in psychology.

> "God's Word speaks into the most painful situations, offering comfort, wisdom, challenge, forgiveness, and hope."

Unfortunately, resources were scarce in war-torn Rwanda. Most mental health professionals had fled the country, if they hadn't been killed. A nation that sorely needed counseling had no counselors.

So this enterprising young woman, spurred on by her own tragic experiences, traveled to Uganda to get a psychology degree—and then returned. She saw trauma everywhere. The needs were overwhelming. What was needed, she determined, was a training program for lay counselors, based in the church.

About that time, Baraka found a book in a library called *Healing the Wounds of Trauma*, published by American Bible Society. This provided the encouragement and guidance she needed to move ahead with her plans. Through this book, she connected with the Trauma Healing Institute at ABS, for which she now serves as an advisor. The nation of Rwanda is slowly recovering from its collective trauma, and Baraka is in the midst of the recovery, training a team of counselors to help others heal.

God's Word speaks into the most painful situations, offering comfort, wisdom, challenge, forgiveness, and hope. For a shell-shocked teenager in Rwanda, for a grieving couple in Ecuador, and for other suffering souls all over the world, the Scriptures unleash the transformative power of God.

I don't mean to make light of the emotional wounds of life. On the contrary. Perhaps you have experienced a soul-numbing tragedy. But within that terrible pain, the Lord can speak to you. When your grief is so deep that it's suffocating you, God's Word is like oxygen pumped directly into your lungs. Even when I was angry at God, I never stopped talking to Him. Even when I

> "Perhaps you have experienced a soul-numbing tragedy. But within that terrible pain, the Lord can speak to you."

didn't know what I was going to do that day, I continued to open His Word and at least try to let it speak to me. And eventually, I started to feel life coming back into my heart. Eventually, Rita could see beyond the darkness of her own pain, gaining enough strength to reach out and help others.

But what about those who cannot read or hear God's Word? When trauma strikes—death, disease, war, terrorism, natural disaster, political or religious repression—what lifeline will they have?

> **"Even when I didn't know what I was going to do that day, I continued to open His Word and at least try to let it speak to me. And eventually, I started to feel life coming back into my heart."**

Those of us in the Bible movement are dedicated to making sure that no person on earth ever has to suffer trauma without access to the Source of all life and hope. Because we know what it is to suffer pain beyond bearing, we are determined that wherever there is suffering, there is also the healing Word of God. We strive to equip Baraka and many others in places of great need, so that they can share the Lord's transformative message.

You're invited to join us in that effort.

Food for Thought

- We all face hardships in our lives, but God promises that He will never leave or forsake us.

- God's Word, spoken through Scripture and fellow believers, can give us comfort and healing during our times of pain.

- As God heals our pain, we can in turn offer God's healing to others.

Questions to Consider

1. What losses have you encountered in your life? How have they affected your relationship with God?

2. Have you ever expressed your honest emotions to God—even your anger? What did you say? If you haven't, what would you say?

3. What is one way you could offer support to someone experiencing similar losses? What is one way you could receive support from someone who has experienced similar losses?

Chapter 11

LEAVING THE JUNGLE, ENTERING THE PALACE

God may indeed reward you with a startling career—
but you will probably not know the details in advance.

Ralph Winter

O ver time, and by the grace and mercy of God, our family began to heal from the trauma and grief of Dean's death. Those who have experienced such a tragic loss will understand when I say that you never actually "get over" such an event; you just learn to live your life around the gaps left by the hole in your life created by the loss of a child. This was certainly true for Rita and me. Gradually, and by different means according to God's slow but steady healing, the two of us moved back into engagement with life and with our work in Ecuador.

I suppose there were times when we thought, "Surely we have weathered the storm; after this, we ought to have clear sailing." We may have entertained such hopes, but it was not to be the case.

Some two years after Dean's death, just as Rita was becoming sufficiently healed to be able to say in her heart, "I believe this is still our place to do God's work," the Quito offices received a shock-

151

ing announcement from the Ecuadorian government: all our personnel had to leave Ecuador within the next six months.

This news sent us reeling, all over again. I was newly in charge of government relations for the work in Ecuador, and I was shocked! God was moving in amazing ways among the tribal peoples of the country; we were so close to our goals for Bible translation for Ecuador that we could nearly reach out and touch them. And now we would have to uproot everything and leave. Had we come to this foreign land, developed new, loving relationships with the people here, and endured the agonizing loss of our son, only to have our passports stamped "nonrenewable" and be shoved toward the exit?

> ". . . you never actually 'get over' such an event; you just learn to live your life around the gaps left by the hole in your life created by [the trauma you have personally experienced]."

Reaching Up, Reaching Out

We went into emergency mode. First, we fell on our knees in prayer, asking God to give us wisdom, perception, and patience in order to do and say what needed to be done and said. Next, we reached out to people in the Ecuadorian government with whom we had developed solid connections during our stay. It soon became clear that this was a public-relations crisis; a radical political faction within the government was instigating lies and opposition to our work.

A highly respected Ecuadorian attorney, a former presidential candidate who also loved the Lord, became a key advocate for us during the ensuing tense debates about our status. He put his reputation on the line by agreeing to host a banquet for government leaders in order to plead our case. At that event, he told them, "These servants should not be thrown out of this country. This would be a disgrace to Ecuador to treat these people that way after all they've done for the ministry to the people groups of this nation."

With our champion leading the way, a number of other legislators stood up and said, "It would be a national travesty if these friends of ours had to leave. They are serving our minority people. They are eliminating illiteracy by teaching our indigenous people to read and to write."

They were right about this; linguists had worked with each language group and developed an alphabet, dictionaries, and reading primers. While it is true that Scripture was often the first thing ever published in the heart language of these people, there were countless other benefits that followed, especially for expanded educational opportunities. Our staff was improving the lives of these hard-to-reach, often neglected tribal groups. Certainly, our work was changing the eternal destiny of each people group, as tribal people were receiving God's Word in their language for the first time, but they were receiving more than that—and our friends in the Ecuadorian government knew it.

But the Enemy never gives ground without a fight. Over the next few weeks, the internal political debates became heated. In the end, an outpouring of goodwill changed the direction, and we were able to complete the work, despite this intense political and spiritual battle.

Meeting with the President

After four years in Ecuador, our work was nearing completion. One of our final official acts before leaving the country was to meet with President Rodrigo Borja. The outcome of this meeting would be pivotal for the continuing work of the workers we would leave behind.

For the occasion we had created a beautiful, custom-made wooden cabinet with glass doors to display copies of books representing all the work that had been done among the people of Ecuador over the past thirty-five years. There were dictionaries, Bibles, primers, Scripture excerpts, and books of songs that had been written in all eight of the languages we had served.

When the day of the presentation arrived, Rita joined us at the presidential palace in Quito to photograph the occasion. We were escorted to a huge hall. Before long, large wooden doors swung open and President Borja and his entourage came to greet us.

As this procession walked toward us, the promise God had given me years earlier flashed through my mind: "Show me someone who does a good job, and I will show you someone who is better than most and worthy of the company of kings" (Proverbs 22:29, GNT). In that moment, I knew without a doubt that I stood in that spot by divine appointment. I knew we would find favor with President Borja, as we had found favor with the people of his nation to whom we had given our lives for the past four years.

It was such an honor to present the president with these samples of our work. When he saw what had been accomplished for his people, he realized the value of Bible translation work in his country.

Not long after this, on May 29, 1992, the Peterson family, celebrating all the goals accomplished, stood in the lobby of the Quito airport, preparing for departure. We fought to control our emotions as we hugged the people who had come to see us off. Rita received an armful of red roses: a beautiful Ecuadorian custom for those leaving the country. The number of friends who gathered to see us off overwhelmed us.

These dear friends had opened their hearts and welcomed us when we arrived. They had helped us through the darkest time of our lives and had stood with us fearlessly for the cause of Bible translation when it could have cost them their careers. They rejoiced with us over the victories, and there had been so many.

Though our prayer and financial partners back in the US were not present that day, they were no less in our hearts. We had been blessed by their faithfulness for the past four years. They had been with us every step of the way and had carried us in prayer on days we didn't think we could keep going. They had made this incredible experience in Ecuador possible. Our lives were richer for it.

That day, as we boarded our flight from Ecuador to the States for a furlough, we felt reasonably prepared for our next assignment— we were invited to a leadership role in Central America. Over the coming months, we decided to serve in Guatemala.

When God Fights for Us

God has always fought for His people. Throughout history, the people of God have been at their strongest when their trust in God has been the deepest. Think about Joshua facing the high, strong walls of Jericho; or young David standing in front of the huge, menacing figure of Goliath; or Peter, James, and John speaking to the Sanhedrin; or even, more recently, Martin Luther King Jr., who refused any longer to turn away from the injustice of racism in the American South and elsewhere.

> "God has always fought for His people. Throughout history, the people of God have been at their strongest when their trust in God has been the deepest."

When people of faith put their trust in God and resolve to stand for Him, no matter the cost, the kingdom of God starts to break down the walls and the chains of "rulers . . . authorities . . . the powers of this dark world," as Paul characterizes the forces that oppose the will of God in Ephesians 6:12. We saw this happen in Ecuador when agitators tried to undermine our Bible translation work there. And others, around the world, have seen it happen, too.

God Makes a Way

One of these witnesses is my friend Pedro Samuc, who grew up in Santiago Atitlán, Guatemala, a small, humble Mayan village on the shore of Lake Atitlán. As a young man, Pedro discovered the importance of mother-tongue Scripture. "Hearing God's Word in the heart language is like the difference between walking into the water or diving deep to find richness and incredible beauty below the surface," Pedro explained. "It's in the depths [of God's Word] that life transformation occurs."

Pedro always looked forward to church, but during the services, he noticed that many of his fellow church members fell asleep. They didn't understand the Spanish language very well, and most of them were manual laborers, tired from the hard workweek. As the service went along in Spanish, it became harder and harder for them to follow along; their eyes became heavy, and it was difficult to pay attention. The church ushers carried long wooden sticks, and when a member dozed off—*whack!* The usher would rap or poke the person with a stick. This disturbed Pedro; it didn't seem to be in keeping with God's love.

He decided to translate some verses of the Bible into Tzútujil, the Mayan dialect spoken in his village. He was sure that if he could share the words of Holy Scripture in the heart language of his people, they would stay awake. With no tools other than his Spanish Bible, a notebook, and a pencil, Pedro began the solitary task of translating verses in the Gospel of John from Spanish into his Mayan language. Soon, he began to encounter opposition; his friends laughed at him, but he persisted.

Actually, Pedro said, he understood the reason for the ridicule. To many, even among the Tzútujil, thought the indigenous culture and language was worthless—something to be ashamed of. Their clothing, their dialect—all of it was considered backward, uncultured, and unworthy of serious consideration. Decades of poverty, illiteracy, and absence of opportunity had convinced Pedro's people that they really were backward, and there was nothing to be done about it.

But Pedro didn't think so. Convinced that his people's lives would be better if they could hear God speaking to them in their own language, he continued translating.

Soon, God led Pedro to a Bible translator who affirmed his work and gave him training. Within a year, Pedro had completed a draft of the entire Gospel of John in Tzútujil—and a strange thing began to happen.

As Pedro translated God's Word, it transformed him. And not only Pedro was changed; those who had previously rejected his translation were now interested. "Pedro, teach us to read and write in our language. Teach us the Bible in Tzútujil," they said.

"This was huge!" Pedro said. Pedro's teaching in the Tzútujil language led to the transformation of many lives; a deep hunger for God's Word increased within the community, and before long, area church leaders began to notice.

When asked to speak at a Tzútujil church event, Pedro was unsure of what might happen. "I started preaching in my native language. I saw changes in the attitude and on the faces. Everybody was paying attention."

No longer were people sleeping in the pews! But not everyone was enthusiastic about Pedro's preaching and teaching in Tzútujil; opposition still remained. Some leaders in the church, for example, were not convinced of the need for mother-tongue translation of God's Word. After all, Spanish, the official language of government and trade in the region, had always been used in the churches. A very important Mayan church leader, many years older than Pedro, was unconvinced that heart-language Scripture had real value, and he questioned Pedro about it.

This was a very delicate situation for Pedro, because in his culture, younger people do not challenge the elders. He spent much time in prayer before responding to the church leader.

When Pedro spoke with the leader, he asked him, "When you were courting your wife, what language did you use? When you said, 'Sweetheart, I love you. I want to be your fiancé,' what language did you use?"

The church leader replied, "I used our Mayan language."

"Why did you use the Mayan language?" Pedro asked.

"Because that is the language that touches her heart. She would understand my intention, that I am concerned for her and that I want her to be my wife."

Pedro said, "Did she understand the language?"

"Of course she understood. That is why she said yes."

"And that is why Jesus wants to speak to His people, His Church, the Bride of Christ, in their heart language: so they will understand His love and care for them," Pedro explained.

> "... Jesus wants to speak to His people, His Church, the Bride of Christ, in their heart language: so they will understand His love and care for them,"

I have never heard a more effective or succinct defense of the importance of heart-language Bible translation. God wants to speak to each of us in the language of our hearts—what could be more natural? Thank God for people like Pedro, who have the courage to persist in the face of ridicule and even opposition from "experts" as they seek to make the Good News accessible to people in a way that most effectively engages their hearts and minds.

A Matter of Life and Death

But Pedro's leadership would not stop with his Bible translation work. Guatemala is a country where political and ethnic differences often lead to violence and repression, and in December 1996, a militia incursion into Pedro's village soon developed into kidnapping, murder, and hostage-taking. Soldiers kicked in the doors of homes, snatching men, women, and children from their beds. "Everyone was frightened," Pedro reported. "They killed almost seventy of us; only ten of us survived in our neighborhood. They set up their headquarters across the street from my house. Night and day they watched us so we couldn't leave the village.

> ". . . the One who created us desires that we live in peace with each other; that the strong act with compassion toward the weak, rather than taking advantage of them."

"One night I heard them kidnapping a neighbor. Thirty minutes later, the townspeople rose up against the assaults; it was chaos. People were screaming, and about 30,000 people had gathered, blocking the army and rescuing the man who had been kidnapped. The army started shooting at the people and ran back to their outpost.

"There were around 20,000 people at the outpost, demanding [that the violence] stop. Then the army captain ordered his men to open fire on [the crowd]. I believe twenty people died, and the total number of hurt and dead was about 500."

Pedro knew something had to be done. "I called the [national] attorney general for human rights, explaining everything. He said he would come, but that the corpses had to be left where they were."

Pedro spread the word, and the townspeople, despite the risk of being shot by the soldiers, prevented the militia from removing the bodies. When the attorney general arrived later that morning, with media in tow, it was the beginning of a national outcry against the violence. Pedro describes it as the beginning of a revolution. In the process, he became known as a man of peace, a leader in the struggle against armed repression.

The Peace Revolution

This is the type of thing that happens when God's Word gains a foothold in the lives of people. Like Pedro, they realize that violence is not the answer. They learn that the One who created us desires that we live in peace with each other; that the strong act with compassion toward the weak, rather than taking advantage of them.

In fact, what I have learned in my years in the Bible movement is this: if you want to change the world, one of the best ways to get started is to connect people with the Word of God in a way that

> ". . . if you want to change the world, one of the best ways to get started is to connect people with the Word of God in a way that engages their minds, imaginations, and hearts."

engages their minds, imaginations, and hearts. Because when people's hearts are transformed, this is only the beginning. There really is no greater transformational power in this world than the living, active Word of God.

Food for Thought

- God has always fought for His people.

- The benefits of heart-language Bible translation do not end with spiritual freedom; they extend to literacy, education, and motivation for positive societal change.

- If you want to change the world, connect people to the Word of God in a way that engages their minds, imaginations, and hearts.

Questions to Consider

1. What do you consider the three greatest needs of society today? How might greater access to God's Word help meet those needs?

2. Have you or someone you know ever intervened in an unjust situation? What happened? How did the teachings of the Bible influence your actions or those of others?

3. How has the Bible engaged your mind, imagination, and heart? How has this engagement impacted your work, relationships, neighborhood, or beyond?

Chapter 12

REACHING THE TOP
BY BEING AT THE BOTTOM

You gotta serve somebody.

Bob Dylan

One day in 1996, I was in my office in Guatemala City, serving now as the field director for operations in Central America, when I received the email from organization headquarters informing staff members around the world that Wycliffe was searching for a new president. I remember glancing over the listed qualifications just before heading out for a meeting. Something about the list really caught my attention.

Later, one of my colleagues in the Guatemala offices said, "Roy, did you see that email from Wycliffe? The qualifications describe you perfectly. Sounds like they're looking for you." I laughed off the comment.

A few days later, as a group of us were praying about the next president for Wycliffe, a friend said, "That position sounds perfect for you." I shook my head. I loved what I was doing in Guatemala and besides, I couldn't imagine a more unlikely scenario.

Still, his words stayed with me. Later, a verse from God's Word spoke to my heart: "In the mouth of two or three witnesses shall every word be established" (2 Corinthians 13:1, KJV). Nevertheless, I was thinking that it would take a whole boatload of witnesses—and a burning bush or two tossed in besides—to convince me to move my family again.

A few weeks later, I flew to the US for a series of international meetings. I walked into a roomful of people, greeted a few I knew, and introduced myself to a few I didn't. Richard Steele heard my voice and called to me above the noise in the room. A valued colleague, Richard is one of the sharpest people I know. At the time, he worked in Braille translation. Though physically blind, Richard has the spiritual vision of a hawk. I walked over to greet him, and he invited me to sit with him and his wife.

"Roy, the Lord has shown me it's you they're looking for," he said. "I have nominated you to be the next president of Wycliffe Bible Translators."

To say I was stunned would be the understatement of the year. These words, coming from Richard, had so much weight. But there were many people much better suited for the job: with better qualifications, more degrees, and superior experience.

"I hope you will let your name stand," Richard said. "I've prayed about it. I believe this is God's doing."

That's when I knew I needed to talk to Rita! I called her during the first break to tell her my name had been submitted.

"You're not going to let your name stand, are you?" she said.

Then I told her about others who had encouraged me. "It seems very unlikely for me to be chosen, though," I said. "Submissions have come in from all over the world; thirty or more people are on the list."

After Rita and I talked, I felt better. We both believed my name would be eliminated quickly. We prayed and trusted Jesus once again.

But when the list dropped from thirty down to ten and my name was still one of them, I called again. "Rita," I said, "we'd better pray harder."

Though I had finished my undergraduate degree in business and was working toward a master's in social science with an emphasis on leadership studies at Azusa Pacific University, the other candidates were far more experientially and academically qualified. Surely they would eliminate me, I thought.

I returned to Guatemala. Weeks passed, and I received a phone call. "We've narrowed it down to three people, Roy," the board member said. "You're one of the three."

As much as I didn't want to leave Guatemala—as much as I didn't *think* I wanted the position—the Lord arrested my heart that day. By this time, I knew He was up to something; I might very well become the next president of Wycliffe Bible Translators.

Rita and I prepared the children for this possibility. We asked Jordan and Corrie to pray about it before we left to meet one final time with the Wycliffe board of directors. They both prayed and gave us their support. By now, Wes had graduated from high school in Guatemala and was attending Moody Bible Institute in Chicago, so we knew he would be fine, whatever the outcome. He eventually went into pastoral ministry. Jordan eventually pursued international business and economics. Corrie became a teacher.

Rita and I sat in a room in Dallas with the other two candidates and their wives, waiting for the board to interview us. We had been in this place before. I remember thinking, *God is going to gently push us out of the boat again!*

After the interviews, the board members convened to vote. We would later learn that they made the decision literally on their knees, in prayer. Each member prayed until he or she believed God had shown the person for the job. Then they took a roll call vote.

"Roy Peterson," said the first one.

"I thought I was the only one picking Roy," said another. "Roy Peterson," said the third and then the fourth . . . and so it went.

When the 11–1 vote was revealed, the loner spoke up. He said he felt led to change his vote to make it unanimous. The board had chosen the wild card—me! Board members reported that the overwhelming presence of God filled the room, giving them all a sense that He was moving in this decision.

Meanwhile, still convinced that we would *not* be chosen, Rita had been out stocking up on bulk quantities of products that she knew, after four years there, were not available back in Guatemala. After the ballots were cast and I gave her the news, Rita just whispered, "Now we pack for California."

Broken Vessels

Rita's calm surrender to this latest movement of God in our lives is a beautiful picture of the way we were both being shaped for service. Going into this leadership role, one thing I knew for certain is that the biblical model of leadership does not feature a big shot in an ivory tower somewhere, ordering minions about. My intention was to serve as Christ served—washing feet, if that was what needed to be done.

Henri Nouwen wrote in his *Life of the Beloved* of how God's preparation of us follows the actions of Jesus as He served His disciples the bread of the Last Supper. Nouwen said we are taken, blessed, broken, and given. God takes us from the world by His sanctifying grace; He blesses us with the Holy Spirit; He breaks us so that we may be offered to all; and then He gives us to the world as a blessing and an extension of His grace.[1]

The third step of Nouwen's description is the hardest, of course. None of us wants to be broken, and yet, just as Christ was broken for us, so we must accept being broken if we are to be useful to God. Walking through the deep valley of grief over Dean's death was certainly a learning experience for living with brokenness.

I remember vividly an occasion, sometime after we lost Dean, when Rita was completing an amazing photography project with the Colorado people in Ecuador. During the course of that assignment, we stayed with some friends in their jungle home for five days. While

> "'. . . God's preparation of us follows the actions of Jesus as He served His disciples the bread of the Last Supper. . . we are taken, blessed, broken, and given. God takes us from the world by His sanctifying grace; He blesses us with the Holy Spirit; He breaks us so that we may be offered to all; and then He gives us to the world as a blessing and an extension of his grace.'"
>
> (Henri J. M. Nouwen)

---

1. Henri J. M. Nouwen, *Life of the Beloved: Spiritual Living in a Secular World* (New York: Crossroad Publishing, 1992).

there, we participated in a worship service in the village, during which Rita was able to share how God had brought her through the heartrending season in our lives that began with Dean's death. Even I was moved by her openness and vulnerability as she described the excruciating path we had walked as we dealt with our anguish. Many were weeping by the time she finished.

For some minutes, the lay pastor conducting the service was unable to speak. When he regained control of his voice, he reflected on the unimaginable pain of losing a son. "And yet God allowed His Son to die for us," he said. Rita's brokenness—and her willingness to share it openly with these believers—had opened another channel for God's saving Word to operate among these tribal people, many of them still like newborn babies in their faith.

One Who Serves

The servanthood model is vital to our work in advancing God's Word across the globe. We make it clear to our local partners in ministry that we want to know how we can best serve them, supporting their efforts on behalf of their own people. It is not our place, we tell them, to move in with them and take over the work. That was the model applied to much of the missionary effort of decades past, and it led too often to the marginalization of local believers. When the ministry of a local people depends too much upon constant infusions from "trained experts," it is too often unable to withstand the onslaughts of the Enemy over the long term.

Instead, we seek to partner with those in each people group whom God has already called. We find out what their needs are and how we may best serve their efforts. In this way, we are serving those who already have the hearts to serve others.

This includes servant-hearted people like Mandowen, a local leader in Bible translation for the Yawa people of Papua New Guinea. Mandowen had a dream one night in which a bird spoke to him, telling him that gold lay at the bottom of the tree in which it was perched. The bird told Mandowen to take the gold to his village. In his dream, he walked through a thick fog to his village, guided by the barely visible figure of someone walking ahead of him.

> "The servanthood model is vital to our work in advancing God's Word across the globe. We seek to partner with those in each people group whom God has already called. We find out what their needs are and how we may best serve their efforts. In this way, we are serving those who already have the hearts to serve others."

Later that day, Mandowen was summoned from working in his family's vegetable patch to meet a visitor who was asking for him. That visitor was Larry Jones, and he had come to ask Mandowen to be part of a Bible translation team.

Mandowen's Yawa people had received teaching years before and many of them were believers, but they had very little Scripture in their heart language.

As one of the very few Yawa who had any advanced education, Mandowen was a natural choice for the translation work. And as soon as he spoke with Larry Jones, he knew that the meaning of his dream was that he should mine for the gold of God's Word and make it available for his people by translating it into their local dialect.

Partners from the United States traveled to Mandowen's village—which had no electricity and certainly no telephones at that time—and installed a solar-powered generator and satellite communications equipment. They also brought Mandowen a specially prepared laptop computer. After a few hours of training, Mandowen was up and running. The pace of his translation work increased greatly with the use of these technological tools.

The Yawa language is very literal. For example, when they pray for understanding or insight, they ask God to "split open" their minds. In 2011, when the Yawa celebrated the dedication of their newly published New Testament, Mandowen sobbed as he told the story of his dream, relating how God had "split open" his mind to understand that he was to take up the work of bringing God's Word to his people in their own language. Today, he teaches in a village school, and the government allows young Yawa children to receive education with materials written in their own language—materials that Mandowen helped develop.

Tough Decisions

Almost as soon as our family arrived at Wycliffe headquarters in California, we faced a difficult challenge. At my very first board meeting as president, the agenda had a single item: deciding whether the organization should remain in California or relocate.

Though the organization had a deep and rich history in its present location—one that reached back at least five decades—we faced significant constraints to our continued growth if we stayed in California. First, the property was landlocked, constraining growth and making it difficult for us to expand our already outgrown facility. Second, the exorbitant cost of living on the West Coast, one mile from the Pacific Ocean, made it difficult to attract the best and brightest, most qualified personnel who could help us position the organization for the future.

This could not be a top-down directive, delivered in an authoritarian management style. On the other hand, my business experience convinced me that in order for the organization to take our proper place in the Great Commission tasks we faced, we had to look at some things differently than we had up to that point. The board was divided, and we knew that many of our dedicated staff and leaders didn't want to leave a place where they had put down deep roots.

We spent a great deal of time in prayer over the matter, and we also kept our eyes and ears open. We initially negotiated for a piece of land in another location; it was certainly large enough to permit us to expand—in fact, it was too large for us to utilize or easily afford.

I contacted ministry CEOs across the country to see if anyone might have an interest in sharing the property with us, since it was really too big for us to handle by ourselves. And then, our negotiation for the property fell through.

At about that same time, however, Dr. Bill Bright, founder and president of Campus Crusade for Christ, and Paul Eshleman, founder of Jesus Film Project, reached out to us and said, "We have an amazing situation. It's very interesting that you would write. We have 1,600 acres in central Florida, and we can't use it all. Would you like 800 of it?" They were offering to share their land!

Our board had established a wish list for any property we would consider occupying, and it was an ambitious list, indeed. The Florida land met every single condition.

I began to suspect that God was edging us toward Florida, and I wasn't very objective. Three of our vice presidents—California-based guys who were not predisposed to move east—went to "spy out the land." Surprisingly to everyone, like Joshua and Caleb, they came home with a glowing report.

Soon, our entire leadership team was on the same page. Then the board voted to move from Orange County, California, to Orange County, Florida. Twelve months later, twenty-seven eighteen-wheelers pulled away from California, headed to Orlando, carrying all the essential cargo for the relocation. Because Campus Crusade (now called simply "Cru" in the US) had rented the buildings for ten years before moving into their own new quarters, we found the amenities already in place. By the fifth day after the arrival of the moving trucks in Orlando, we had computers online, phones connected, and our vision for the future moving ahead at full speed. With new partnerships, a new structure, and a new strategic plan, Wycliffe Bible Translators was getting positioned for the twenty-first century.

Accepting the Unexpected

A friend of mine once quipped, "It's very difficult to make accurate predictions, especially about the future." Can you relate? But one thing I have learned—and am still learning—is that God weaves the unexpected very skillfully into the ever-expanding tapestry of His will. What we do not understand or even struggle with today often bears fruit for the kingdom tomorrow. Our brokenness at Dean's death equipped us with reserves of compassion that God has used for His glory. The challenges I faced as I assumed leadership ushered in new opportunities for growth and service. And

> ". . . one thing I have learned—and am still learning—is that God weaves the unexpected very skillfully into the ever-expanding tapestry of His will. What we do not understand or even struggle with today often bears fruit for the kingdom tomorrow."

within a few years, we would grapple once again with the surprising twists and turns, seeing God not yet done inviting us to the unexpected.

Food for Thought

- Our worldly qualifications are not a hindrance to God; God accomplishes His purposes even in the most unlikely scenarios.

- We are called to serve as Christ served, from washing feet to empowering others in effective ministry.

- What we do not understand today, or even what we struggle with, often bears fruit for the kingdom tomorrow.

Questions to Consider

1. Have you ever received confirmation through other people? What did they tell you? Did their words give you assurance to take action?

2. How can our brokenness help us serve others? What might we learn from the experience of being broken that we could not learn otherwise?

3. What events in your life were difficult to understand at the time but have since borne fruit? How has this given you a different perspective on the past?

Chapter 13

ANOTHER SURPRISE BEGINNING

---

*Am I open to the God of surprises? Am I a person
who stands still, or a person on a journey?*

Pope Francis

By 2002, we were moving Wycliffe out of the "temporary" location that we had rented from Cru and into beautiful, new, permanent headquarters in Orlando. We had a dream to dedicate the building debt-free and to see God fill it with people who were passionate about getting His Word translated into every known language. The project cost more than $40 million and a lot of faith to see this happen. By now, $38 million had come in, and we were down to a remaining need of $2 million.

About this same time, God began drawing Rita and me into a more concentrated time of prayer. Following the example of our friends Bill and Vonette Bright, the founders of Cru, we committed to forty days of prayer and a Daniel Fast, a modified fasting method, as we focused our hearts on discerning God's will for our lives.

We should have known that when you earnestly seek God's guidance, He will often take you in unexpected directions. I suppose, given our lives up to this point, Rita and I ought to have been at least somewhat prepared for yet another surprise change in our plans, as Pope Francis mentions in the quote above.[1] After all, we had, in the course of the previous few years, sold a newly built house in Guatemala City where we thought we'd live for years in order to move to California, then in less than twenty-four months sold a house in California in order to move to Orlando—all in response to God's leading. All of this reminds me of the Jewish proverb: "If you want to make God laugh, tell Him your plans." But even with all this, as Rita and I went into this forty-day period focused on spiritual discernment, six years into this new role, I don't think either of us anticipated what was about to happen.

Rita, as is her usual practice, dove in with all her heart, and she began hearing from God before I did. I would come home and find her weeping and struggling with God in a way that baffled me. She would be in the middle of a wrenching spiritual experience, sensing God challenging her to *let go* of things—everything. She would tell me how God dealt with her about *giving up* something or someone, trusting this person to God. He was talking to her about trusting Him totally with our children and our new grand-daughter, Juliana, the first child of our son Wes and his wife, Jama. God also asked her to give up other things important to her, including our home in Orlando. Rita was hearing things in her spirit that made no sense to her, or me—until we reached Day 28 of our fast.

At this time, in addition to serving as president of Wycliffe, I was also on the board of The Seed Company, a small startup organization, founded by Bernie May, one of the most energetic,

---

1. Ann Schneible, "God Is a God of Surprises, Pope Francis Preaches," *Catholic News Agency* [online], October 13, 2014. Available at http://www.catholicnewsagency .com/news/god-is-a-god-of-surprises-pope-preaches-50141/ (accessed June 28, 2016).

visionary, and faithful people I have ever met during my time in the Bible movement. In 1993, Bernie stepped out of the president's office at Wycliffe and into a converted broom closet that would serve as his "office." With a phone, a desk, and the help of a single volunteer—Marguerite, his longtime assistant—he set about praying and working to develop new strategies for creating, fostering, and strengthening on-the-ground partnerships with locally led translation groups to accelerate the rate of Bible translation around the world. He was sixty years old at the time. He prayed, "Lord, if You'll give me ten years, I'd like to help 200 indigenous translation teams get Your Word for their people groups."

Now, ten years and 200 successful translations later, Bernie was retiring. The Seed Company board of directors was coming to Orlando, meeting to discuss the question on everyone's mind: Who would replace Bernie May?

A Seed Is Planted

Thus it was that, on Day 28 of Rita's and my time of prayer and fasting, I was up before dawn and starting my morning exercise. I immediately began talking to God about the miracle we needed to dedicate the new headquarters building debt-free. Then, God started pointing me toward The Seed Company and a replacement for Bernie. So, I began praying in that direction.

Suddenly, I had a vivid mental picture: I was at The Seed Company in the midst of a surge of translation activity, and God was doing absolutely amazing things. I saw The Seed Company helping a staggering number of people groups, and I was there serving.

Why would I be at The Seed Company? I thought. *I'm the president of Wycliffe, and I'm on their board.*

Though it was just a quick flash, a very strong impression lingered. I'd had enough encounters with the Lord to know that this might be from Him. What should I do with this experience?

When I got back home from my walk, Rita was just waking up, still sleepy. I slid the news in sideways. "Oh, by the way, honey, I think the Lord has been talking to me about The Seed Company. I might need to make myself available. Nothing to worry about, though."

She mumbled, "Okay, if that's what the Lord says."

Promptly at 7:30 a.m., Wycliffe attorney Bob Lipps, a trusted colleague and also a good friend, picked me up for The Seed Company board meeting.

"So, Roy, what's the Lord been showing you during your fast?"

I gave him something vague. "Oh, I'm reading and learning about . . ."

"No, Roy. What's He saying about *you*? Do you see any change coming?"

Silence. I'm feeling much too vulnerable about sharing.

"Has the Lord shown you anything about going to The Seed Company?"

Bam! There it was, right out in the open. We hadn't even made it to the end of the block.

"Where did that come from, Bob? Why are you asking that question?"

Bob said he didn't know why he asked me that question. Then, as I related to him my experience from earlier that morning, I saw the blood drain from his face.

Here's what I was thinking: the Wycliffe board was weeks away from electing me to my third term in the role of president, for three more years of service; we were at the end of an intense building campaign, needing the final $2 million to dedicate our building debt-free; our daughter, Corrie, was headed for college, here in Florida; Wes, his wife, and our first grandbaby were nearby in Tampa; Rita had painted the walls and hung curtains in our new home.

It didn't seem like a logical time to pull up stakes. Then again, it never does.

"Roy, you need to tell The Seed Company board."

I looked at Bob and shook my head. I didn't think I was ready for that step.

"At least tell the chairman, Peter Ochs," he said.

That seemed better. I could do that. After all, Peter, the chairman of the board, was a very wise and trusted friend. He might just shrug it off.

But he didn't shrug. Instead, Peter insisted that I share my experience with the rest of the board.

When they heard the news, they felt God had answered their prayers. Founding board member Rick Alvord then related that as he had boarded the plane to come to the Florida for the meeting that day, he had a picture in his mind for the next CEO of The Seed Company. He pictured me—and then promptly dismissed it as impossible. After all, I was president of Wycliffe!

As we celebrated a strong sense of God's direction, I was remembering that I told Rita that morning not to worry.

After only four years, we'd left Guatemala before our new home there was finished and had begun planning our departure from California before the shipping crates from Guatemala were unpacked.

Now after only six years we were days away from dedicating the new Wycliffe building in Orlando, and God was calling us to The Seed Company in Arlington, Texas.

While those around me were rejoicing, all I could think was, *I've got to talk to Rita.*

I prayed a little harder.

I suppose I shouldn't have fretted. After all, things just seem to fall into place when we say yes to God.

Of course, to be completely fair, the Wycliffe board of directors struggled with the news, but over time they also sensed that my move to The Seed Company was something God was doing. And at the last minute, Corrie decided to attend college in Texas instead of staying in Florida. Finally, on Day 39 of our fast, the last $2 million miraculously came in for the new building.

On Day 40, we stood at the dedication for the Wycliffe USA headquarters in Orlando, knowing in our hearts that God had used us to accomplish what He had sent us to do. As soon as the fledgling Seed Company in Southern California decided where to set up their new headquarters in Texas, the Petersons would be on the move again.

Rita, of course, was ready. She had given all these things over to the Lord before Day 28 of the fast.

What Matters Most

At this point, those of you keeping score at home may be thinking something along the lines of, "Can't he keep a job?" Or, "What is it with this downwardly mobile guy? He rises through the ranks at American Greetings, and just as he is in line for a nice promotion, he jumps ship to start all over as a missionary. Then, when he finally gets to the top of one of the most respected and effective missions organizations in the world, he takes another exit, going to work at a startup that is actually a tiny affiliate of the company of which he is president. And oh, by the way, he has walked away from a string of real estate that stretches from Florida, to Central America, to the West Coast, and back to where he started."

Trust me: I've stood back, looked at myself, and had many of those same observations. The only way I can explain it is this: ever since I was rescued in that Mexican prison by reading God's Word in my own language, the central passion of my life has been making that same experience available to others. To me, nothing else matters as much as that.

> "True success has nothing to do with position, title, or privilege, and it certainly has nothing to do with institutional perpetuation. Instead, success lies in pursuing the mission toward which your passion is leading you."

The only reason I resigned from American Greetings to join Wycliffe was because of that passion, shared by my faithful and godly wife. When I became president of Wycliffe—much to my surprise, as I've told you—my only purpose was to serve that mission by better empowering Wycliffe to pursue its commitment to the Great Commission.

And now, I realized that leading The Seed Company in its pursuit of local translation partnerships was the best way, at that time in my life, to further that overarching mission. If I have learned one thing during this amazing ride that God has taken me on, it is this: True success has nothing to do with position, title, or privilege, and it certainly has nothing to do with institutional perpetuation. Instead, success lies in pursuing the mission toward which your passion is leading you. That passion—placed in my heart by God—was leading me again. It was time for me to surrender to God's gentle push.

I think that sometimes, when we read about the great heroes of faith, either in the Bible or in church history, we tend to focus only on their great accomplishments. We look at Paul and think of his bold missionary journeys, of the many churches he planted and nourished all across the Roman Empire, of the inspired epistles he wrote that form the underpinning of so much of Christian doctrine and practice. We look at Martin Luther and see the great, liberating tide of the Protestant Reformation that he helped unleash across Europe.

But we don't see all that Paul gave up in order to take hold of what the Lord was calling him toward. We don't see his old teacher, Gamaliel, shaking his head with worry about the way his star rabbinic pupil was placing himself at odds with a religious group that had previously been grooming him for leadership. We don't feel the loneliness in the heart of Luther as he realized that, in order to follow the God-given conviction of his heart, he was going to have to go against the teachings of the church, as it had existed for centuries, all the way up to this day.

I believe that every single person who has ever been used by God to accomplish something great for the kingdom has had to make that momentous, breathtaking choice: to let go of something that is known and trusted in order to lay hold of something unknown and untried that has the potential, with God's help, to make an impact on our world.

As my family prepared to make yet another move in order to follow God's insistent call, we acted in the belief that leaping through the air into God's arms is ultimately safer than standing on the ledge. The ledge may feel more secure for the moment, but in God's arms, we are carried to places we could never have dreamed we would go.

> "I believe that every single person who has ever been used by God to accomplish something great for the kingdom has had to make that momentous, breathtaking choice: to let go of something that is known and trusted in order to lay hold of something unknown and untried that has the potential, with God's help, to make an impact on our world."

Food for Thought

- The greatest sensitivity to God's leading is developed through fervent prayer and attention to the promptings of His Spirit.

- Success lies in pursuing the mission toward which your passion is leading you.

- To be used mightily for God's kingdom we have to make a choice: to let go of what is known and lay hold of what is unknown but has the potential to change the world.

Questions to Consider

1. What would you have to lay on the altar to follow God? What relationships, dreams, or habits are hard to let go of and entrust to God?

2. Has making God your central passion ever reordered your priorities? What did you have to say "no" to in order to say "yes" to God?

3. If you received what you thought was a prompting from God, how might you go about trying to verify it? Would you try fasting, seeking outside counsel, or different forms of prayer?

Chapter 14

TABLE 71

A man may do an immense deal of good,
if he does not care who gets the credit for it.

Father Strickland

I can look back now and see that God was preparing my heart for the move to The Seed Company at least two years prior to the events I've just described in the previous chapter. Really, it all started at Table 71.

In 2000, the Billy Graham Evangelistic Association sponsored the World Congress on Evangelism at Amsterdam, as it had done three times before: at Berlin (then West Berlin) in 1966; at Lausanne, Switzerland, in 1974 (Lausanne I), and at Manila in 1989 (often called "Lausanne II"). These three previous events—and especially Lausanne I—have been commonly recognized as watersheds for interdenominational cooperation in reaching the entire world with the Gospel.

The Amsterdam event would prove just as pivotal, especially for those of us in the world Bible movement. At the time I was still president of Wycliffe, and Rita and I were privileged to be in attendance. Our focus was identifying and reaching the *unreached, unengaged people groups* (UUPGs): those who have no Scripture in their own heart language, who do not have access to a church, and who probably have not heard the Gospel. Our goal was to encourage attendees to join us in starting one hundred new translations. We prayed earnestly to connect with evangelists from around the world who would help reach one hundred people groups.

To my surprise, I didn't have to motivate anyone. Evangelists came forward, pleading with us to help them get Scriptures translated into their languages.

Bruce Wilkinson, Christian leader and founder of Walk Thru the Bible, was the master of ceremonies for the event. At Billy Graham's request, Paul Eshleman, vice president of networks and partnerships for Campus Crusade and founder of the Jesus Film Project, convened the meetings.

Setting the Stage

The highlight of the entire conference took place on the third day of the gathering. Little did we know the surprise God had in store as Bruce opened that session with these words: "Let's begin now, today, to make a commitment that our own organizations—those represented in this room—will reach the unreached peoples of the world."

The people attending represented thousands of missionaries and billions of dollars of resources. Bruce pointed out that there were 252 unreached groups of at least 100,000 people: "ethnic groups that had never been engaged with the Gospel in all of Church history." Bruce also explained that, at that time, approximately 3,000 people groups still needed God's Word in their language, beyond the more than 1,000 languages where a work was in progress. He explained that at the current rate of translation, more than a billion people would

TABLE 71

be lacking the whole Bible for another 100 to 150 years. "That's too long to wait," he said. "So let's start signing up now."

Then it happened: here and there, leaders of ministries stood up to make commitments.

"I'll take responsibility for this people group," someone said.

"We'll take these two," another said.

Someone waved and said, "Our organization will take these five."

The room erupted! For at least half an hour, the noise-filled room was bustling with excitement. Leaders of major organizations were making strategic decisions to mobilize resources for prayer, funding, and growth, and making tactical decisions on where people should be assigned. People were praying and raising hands to sign up. Leaders were going to Paul Eshleman and making commitments. It was a joyous event to see the enthusiasm race through the room of more than 500 leaders, seated and standing around the 75 numbered tables.

And then the action stopped. No one else came up; no one else raised a hand. Of the 252 UUPGs of more than 100,000 people, only 140 had been spoken for. "There shouldn't be any people groups left," Bruce said.

Still, no one moved. There were 112 people groups left.

"God, You don't do things halfway," he said. Then he sat on the platform and prayed silently.

The only noise in the room was coming from Table 71—right across from me—and they were abuzz. Someone from that table said, "Why don't we just take the rest?"

People representing some impressive organizations were seated at Table 71: Campus Crusade for Christ, Youth with a Mission (YWAM), and the International Mission Board (IMB) of the Southern Baptist Convention. Meanwhile, up on the platform, Bruce was still praying.

"Roy," someone said to me, "we're thinking if we form a coalition as a group of ministries in cooperation, then all of our skill sets and products complement one another. We could take the rest of the UUPGs of more than 100,000 population."

I didn't hesitate. "I'm all in," I said as I committed for Wycliffe. Mark Anderson, with YWAM, said, "We're in."

> "The cooperation forged that day—across denominational and confessional lines, across different areas of ministry, across varying organizational concentrations—was the starting point for an unprecedented leap forward in eliminating worldwide Bible poverty in our day."

"Us too," said Avery Willis with the International Mission Board.

Steve Douglass, the new President of Campus Crusade (Cru), said, "We will be taking the Gospel to the most unreached places on earth."

All of us around Table 71 agreed, and then we raised our hands and said to Bruce, up on the platform, "We'll take the rest of the groups."

I still get teary-eyed when I think of how it felt to experience that moment, when God was moving in the hearts and imaginations of those of us in that room in Amsterdam. We knew that we were poised on the brink of something extraordinary. The cooperation forged that day—across denominational and confessional lines, across different areas of ministry, across varying organizational concentrations—was the starting point for an unprecedented leap forward in eliminating worldwide Bible poverty in our day.

TABLE 71

Maintaining Momentum

Since that initial gathering in 2000, over 90 percent of the largest UUPGs have been reached with the Gospel, or somebody is on the ground, working to help reach them. Table 71 has been so effective that in 2010 we moved to the next level and began targeting people groups of 50,000 to 99,000 people. As of 2013, we had a new list of 600 to 700 UUPGs we want to reach. To this day, over sixteen years now, this same group still meets together as Table 71. We convene quarterly to strategize and seek God about how to engage more languages and more UUPGs in Bible translation.

That's our focus, and we're doing it together. We have purposely not created an organization. We haven't tried to raise money or grow in number. However, we have grown together as we've watched God work in our lives and organizations. God has helped us discover what He can do when committed people agree in purpose and are willing to throw all the credit His way.

Another outgrowth of Table 71 is the Call2All Movement (C2A). Mark Anderson became president of C2A in 2007, honing in on the need to call all Christian leaders all over the world to join in fulfilling the Great Commission. Since the first gathering of the group in 2008, more than 1,400 organizations that include some 28,000 global Christian leaders have joined in rallying the worldwide church to collaborate in carrying out Jesus' final instructions to his followers: "Go and teach all nations."

Stronger Together

In many ways, what we experienced that day at Table 71 bears out the wisdom of Paul's teaching about the body of Christ. As Paul explains in 1 Corinthians 12, the body functions best when each part does its work as it is designed to do: the eye provides vision; the hand does the work; the legs carry the body from one place to another. As one of my Table 71 fellows said to me that day, "Our skill sets and products complement one another." It is so true that when we focus on our shared goal—providing Bible access and engagement to those who don't have it—and combine our varied strengths and capabilities, we accomplish so much more together than any of us could alone. We truly become greater than the sum of our parts.

> ". . . when we focus on our shared goal—providing Bible access and engagement to those who don't have it—and combine our varied strengths and capabilities, we accomplish so much more together than any of us could alone. We truly become greater than the sum of our parts."

As a result of Table 71, we have determined upon a goal of reaching every remaining people group by the year 2025. This is, in many ways, an audacious goal. Consider that in the roughly two thousand years of Bible translation, production, and distribution, we have only provided the entire Bible for a portion of the 7,000 known

TABLE 71

language groups. How can we possibly expect to reach everyone else that's left—in less than ten years?

I believe we will reach this goal because God is empowering the effort, and because His people are committed to doing whatever He asks in service to that effort. If it were not possible for us to reach "all the world" with the Gospel, Jesus would never have asked us to do it. But it is His will that the whole world hear the Good News—in words that each can understand—and therefore, I believe that it will happen, in our lifetime.

A Seed Falls into the Ground

Bernie May, the founder of The Seed Company, believed it, too. As he moved into his "broom closet office," he was charged with developing a strategy to accelerate the rate of worldwide Bible translation. Once Bernie hit upon the idea of partnering with indigenous translation teams, he identified ten people groups in the world with at least one person capable of beginning the translation work, with financial and logistical assistance from The Seed Group and its backers.

His biggest challenge in those early days was what he called "the chicken-egg problem": "You can't really connect a financial partner with a translation project until you have a project," Bernie explained. "And you can't get anything going with a project until you have a financial partner."

One day Bernie received a call from Ken Taylor, founder of Tyndale Publishing House. "You know, I've heard about what you're doing," Taylor said. "I really would like to talk to you. Could you come by and see me?"

Bernie went. He shared the vision. Ken told him, "Bernie, this makes great sense to me. Go for it." Ken was already convinced of the need for Bible translation into the heart languages. Also, Ken believed indigenous people could and should be the translators. After all, that is what he had done with *The Living Bible.*

"I just want to encourage you," Ken said. Then he told Bernie he also wanted to support the work financially. With that, Tyndale House became the first major investor for The Seed Company's vision to accelerate Bible translation through partnering with nationals.

With the seed money secured, Bernie was able to attract additional backers to fund the ten test projects to completion. Indigenous-led Bible translation was launched, thanks to God bringing together Bernie's passion and vision with Ken Taylor's faith and resources, proving once again that we are more capable in concert with others than we are individually.

A few years later, as I left the presidency of Wycliffe to begin my work with The Seed Company, I was very conscious of having some big shoes to fill. Bernie May's vision, passion, and commitment to faithful service were legendary. But I also had a profound confidence in the strategy that he had put in place for planting indigenous movements of Bible translation in the world's hardest-to-reach places. I knew that God would nurture those seeds to bear much fruit for the kingdom, and I wanted to do whatever I could to facilitate their growth and even wider dissemination.

My experiences at Table 71 had convinced me of the validity of dreaming big dreams for God. The next decade would afford me unforgettable experiences as I saw so many of those dreams become reality.

TABLE 71

This has become a recurring experience in my life. Again and again, I've seen "Table 71" moments when people of vision responded to overwhelming needs with audacious faith. At The Seed Company and now at American Bible Society, I've been surrounded by people with God-shaped hearts, God-sized dreams, and God-given courage.

Over the last few decades, many Christians have grown alarmed at America's slide away from the Bible, church, and faith. But what could we do about it?

With American Bible Society's move to Independence Mall in Philadelphia, a new vision began to emerge. We suddenly found ourselves in a hot spot for tourists—but more than that, it's a place where Americans come to connect with their national heritage. *What does it mean to be an American? How did this all happen? And what's our inheritance of this, even today?*

> "Again and again, I've seen "Table 71" moments when people of vision responded to overwhelming needs with audacious faith."

Visitors are inspired by the Liberty Bell, Independence Hall, and the Constitution Center. Hearing about the exploits of Washington, Franklin, Jefferson, and many others, these tourists connect deeply with the story of America's founding. But could we fill in a critical and missing part of that story?

That question began to captivate a growing team of visionaries at ABS. We knew that the Bible was an important part of this first American experiment, often quoted by America's founders. The values they fought for were rooted in Scripture.

Could we create a go-to destination for tourists that would stand beside Independence Hall and the Liberty Bell and remind them of the Bible's role in America's founding?

"With American Bible Society's move to Independence Mall in Philadelphia, a new vision began to emerge. We suddenly found ourselves in a hot spot for tourists—but more than that, it's a place where Americans come to connect with their national heritage. *What does it mean to be an American? How did this all happen? And what's our inheritance of this, even today?*"

That in itself was a big dream, but it got bigger. This place would have to compete with dozens of other Philadelphia attractions. We would need state-of-the-art displays, attractive designs, cool technology, the best in market research. What's more, we recognized that we couldn't just preach to visitors. We needed to invite them into an experience of discovery that might lead to lasting Scripture engagement long after they left our building.

We call it the Faith and Liberty Discovery Center. Not a museum, but an experience. People will not only learn how the Bible inspired the signers of the Declaration, but they'll see how Americans through the centuries have sought to apply Scripture to everyday challenges—from William Penn to Martin Luther King, Jr. They'll walk into a room, don special goggles, and see an augmented reality—an image of George Whitefield preaching on that

TABLE 71

site or Abigail Adams sending Scripture verses to her husband, John. As they stroll through the various exhibits, they'll each carry a "page of inspiration"—a tablet-like device that will collect the information they find most meaningful and automatically send it to their phones or home computers. In this way, they can remember their visit—and also come back to the Scriptures they discovered along the way.

These technological advances remind me of how fast our world is changing. We have no time for timidity. As we seek to serve the Lord effectively in the twenty-first

> "As we seek to serve the Lord effectively in the twenty-first century, we need to venture forth and find cutting-edge solutions to age-old challenges. More than anything, we need to be willing to dream the big dreams God gives us."

century, we need to venture forth and find cutting-edge solutions to age-old challenges.

More than anything, we need to be willing to dream the big dreams God gives us.

Food for Thought

- When the various parts of the body of Christ work together, the result is greater than anything they can achieve alone.

- Commitment and conviction are contagious.

- When we join with others to dream big for God, our dreams can become a reality.

Questions to Consider

1. Have you ever been present in a group when God's Spirit was actively accomplishing a higher purpose? What first made you realize that God was moving? What happened as a result? If you have not had such an experience, what do you imagine it would be like?

2. What positive experiences have you had with collaboration? What different skills or gifts did people contribute? How did your differences work together to accomplish your goal?

3. What big dreams do you have for God's kingdom? If you could do anything, what would it be? Where would you go? Who would it involve?

Chapter 15

SEEDS OF SUCCESS

But some seeds fell in good soil, and the plants bore grain:
some had one hundred grains, others sixty, and others thirty.

Matthew 13:8, GNT

I n 2003, when I took over as president and CEO of The Seed Company, things were lining up globally to accelerate the pace of Bible translation beyond our wildest dreams. Inspired ideas and creative concepts that had been simmering on the back burner would soon take off. God was moving people into strategic positions, strengthening bonds within the ranks, and handpicking new partners to work together to get the job done.

As I assumed the leadership, I knew that I wanted to focus on the concept of partnership that Bernie May had pioneered, locating indigenous translation teams with which The Seed Company could come alongside, providing resources to facilitate the work that was already being done in the heart language of the team members. "We're not going to live in your community," Bernie would tell his national partners. "We're not going to do the work. But we'll help you. Tell us how we can serve you. What do you need to get the job done?"

In the spirit and philosophy of Table 71, I wanted to extend this partnership philosophy even further. I knew that within the global church lived committed, mission-minded people with skills, knowledge, capabilities, and resources that could increase Bible access and engagement around the world. And I knew that many of these people were just as interested as I was in breaking down the silos and releasing the power of spiritual synergy as we cooperated to take the Good News to every corner of the earth. International partners like Bible Translation and Literacy in Nairobi, Kartidaya in Jakarta, and Davar in Israel; and US-based ministries like T4 Global in Dallas, the Jesus Film Project in Orlando, and Faith Comes by Hearing in Albuquerque were eager to join hands as we all combined our various gifts and passions to take God's Word to places it had never been.

> "God brought strategic innovations and creative ideas to the forefront: pilot projects with great potential: some new, some tried-and-true strategies with a new twist, and some forward-thinking ideas."

God brought strategic innovations and creative ideas to the forefront: pilot projects with great potential: some new, some tried-and-true strategies with a new twist, and some forward-thinking ideas. I reminded myself that our very wise founding board chairman, Peter Ochs, had given us permission to take chances, stressing that we must assume some calculated risks to discover new ways to do things and test new ideas. "You cannot have an innovative environment where mistakes are punished and where risk is not tolerated," he said. "It kills innovation."

It was a heady time; a spirit of innovation and excitement permeated our hearts and minds. And as we began to hone our strategy for the new millennium, we soon became focused on three central initiatives: the Luke Partnership and the Jesus Film, "cluster" translation projects, and oral culture and storytelling.

Beginning with Chairman Peter Ochs, a highlight of these years was a progressive board of business and ministry leaders who helped create such a dynamic, fast-growing organization. After Peter's term of service ended, Judy Sweeney, Todd Peterson, and Rick Britton all made enormous contributions, from their respective successful careers in the business world.

The Luke Partnership and the Jesus Film

In 1999, Paul Eshleman, founder of the Jesus Film Project, had posed an important question to The Seed Company, still led at that time by Bernie May: "How can we get Bible translations started more quickly where there is no Scripture and no Jesus Film?"

The Jesus Film, based on the life of Christ, is scripted in its entirety from the verses of the English Version of the Gospel of Luke, a provision from American Bible Society. First released in 1979 with the script provided by ABS, the goal of the project was to reach every people group on earth with the story of Jesus in its own language through video/audio media. Although the Jesus Film was already impacting people groups across the globe, the organization had hit a roadblock for thirty of the world's largest unreached language groups in the world. The problem? There was no translation of Luke's Gospel or any Scripture at all in those languages.

Before they could script the film, they needed the translation of Luke. It was recommended to Paul that he contact The Seed Company, which he did. As I was getting up to speed in my new role, I sensed shared excitement about the potential for this partnership, but we also realized that it involved a completely new project design that included more direct involvement with field partners shaping project design as we focused on the translation of Luke's Gospel.

Incidentally, Paul Eshleman and his group had learned something important in their work, a fact that speaks directly to the importance of heart-language translation. Their post-viewing surveys of audiences for the film clearly demonstrated that viewers who saw the Jesus Film in their local dialect had a positive response rate four times greater than those who viewed it in a national or trade language. My own experience confirms this; when people see the dramatic images, and then when they hear Jesus speaking in their heart language, they exclaim, "Jesus speaks our language!" Lives are changed as a result, and that is what drives the entire effort and makes it worthwhile. "People shouldn't have to learn another language to hear the Gospel," Paul said—and he is absolutely right.

So, when Paul came to ask if we could move thirty of his projects to the top of our priority list, we already knew that this was a wonderful fit with our own mission. Still, we had to pause. After all, there were important reasons why these particular thirty translations had never been done. Most were in very isolated, hard-to-reach locations, or else in areas where Christians were being persecuted.

But ultimately, we jumped in with both feet. We knew that the potential impact was tremendous and that we would gain important opportunities for interaction with local churches. This, in turn, would give us crucial information about the need for Scripture translation in these areas.

Nevertheless, this was a job that called for a highly qualified person to handle the sensitive situations that would inevitably occur when working in the type of areas where we would be involved. As far as we were concerned, there was only one person for the job: Katy Barnwell.

Dr. Barnwell is a global treasure, an icon in the world of international Bible translation. At the time we approached her, she brought thirty-five years of field experience in some of the world's most sensitive areas. "Would you consider joining this partnership with the Jesus Film Project to help us complete this work?" we asked her. She accepted.

"The Jesus Film group didn't waste time giving us a list of priority languages," Katy recalled. "Many languages were in hard-to-reach places, where we thought there was no Christian presence. Many looked impossible at first. But then God gave us one contact, which led to another contact, and so on. If God hadn't opened doors, we could not have done the work. That was key."

Many global missions experts have cited the Jesus Film as one of the most powerful evangelistic tools of the modern age. With 6 billion viewings worldwide since 1979, more than 200 million people are estimated to have received Christ as their personal Savior after watching it. What a privilege it is for American Bible Society to have provided the Scripture text for the Jesus Film script!

The Luke Partnership, in turn, uniting the Jesus Film and Bible translation, has been extremely effective. Bill Wolfe, director of global partnerships with the Jesus Film Project said recently, "Our Luke partnership is even more critical now than when we first started. We're totally dependent upon Bible translators to do their work so we can produce the film." As for the Bible translation movement, our partnership with the Jesus Film Project launched us toward greater acceleration of Bible translation and seeing more and more people come into the kingdom of God.

It was a God-inspired plan. God was out front, preparing the way. He brought in new indigenous partners to work with us. He also gave us new ideas. "Could we group similar languages together during training workshops?" someone asked. "Could we train translators from similar, but different, languages in a group at the same time?" We decided to try it, and this effort would prove to be the second game-changer.

"Cluster" Translation Projects

We tested this idea first with a few languages in Ethiopia, Madagascar, and Asia. Then Katy began to look at Nigeria. "We had an invitation from Anglican Bishop Henry Ndukuba of the Gombe Diocese," Katy said. "He was anxious to see translation done in several languages of his diocese."

This would become a historic development: the first time in Nigeria that speakers from numerous languages would be "clustered" together to tackle Bible translation. Seven groups came. The Nigeria Gombe Cluster project of ten languages emerged, and God brought our friends Alan and Kathrine Barnhart as strategic partners.

This concept of conducting translation workshops with a cluster of languages not only would bring God's Word to more languages, it would also make Bible translation possible for the smallest people groups on earth: many of them tucked away in rainforests, on mountaintops, on remote islands, or beyond the farthest reach of desert lands.

Remembering Christ's own commitment to all people, no matter how large their language group, we called people groups with fewer than 10,000 speakers the "Least of These." There are over 1,000 of these people groups without Scripture in their language.

One good example of a Least of These project is a thirteen-language cluster in the Amazon in Brazil. Seven of the languages have only a few hundred speakers, the smallest three having 300 each. All twelve languages have joined hands with the Chibi, a "big sister" people group of 800,000, making Bible translation possible for the "little guys" at a greatly reduced cost. Look at God!

Today the cluster concept is advancing Bible translation by combining the skills of local speakers working together to translate Scripture into their unique, yet related, languages.

"... Bible translation often opens the door for literacy and education. It promotes biblical esteem and helps affirm the unique identity of a people group. Heart-language Scripture helps preserve the culture of these often forgotten or marginalized people groups that get lost in today's globalization."

It's not unusual for Scripture to be the first *written* text in a language. Many people groups who don't have access to God's Word are still oral communities; there is no written form of their language.

But as we have seen time and again, Bible translation often opens the door for literacy and education. It promotes biblical esteem and helps affirm the unique identity of a people group. Heart-language Scripture helps preserve the culture of these often forgotten or marginalized people groups that get lost in today's globalization.

Thanks to this second, game-changing strategy of small people groups working together in related-language clusters to translate Scripture, we are moving rapidly toward our goal to see God's Word in every language, in this generation.

Oral Culture and Storytelling

At the same time the Jesus Film partnership and cluster translation projects were on the rise, a third strategy came into focus. This initiative, involving a technique that is both timeless and new, would help change the face of Bible translation.

> "Thanks to this second, game-changing strategy of small people groups working together in related-language clusters to translate Scripture, we are moving rapidly toward our goal to see God's Word in every language, in this generation."

We shouldn't be surprised that one of the most powerful methods for getting God's Word into the hearts of Bible-less people groups today is the same method Jesus used 2,000 years ago.

Jesus told stories. He didn't pass out pamphlets or Bibles. There were no printed texts to distribute, no video or audio—just oral stories. Jesus took every opportunity to bring people closer to the

Father. Whether speaking to a multitude on a hillside, a roomful of disciples, or a child on His knee, He often told parables. In fact, a well-known preacher once said, "Jesus was God, telling stories."

In 2003, we began focusing more intentionally on translation for oral Bible storytelling. With more than 50 percent of the world's population living in oral cultures, most with no written form of their language, this approach is perfect for quickly bringing God's Word to men, women, and children in some of the world's most remote, backward places.

Bible stories are crafted directly from translated Scripture. While these stories are translated with precision and expertise, they're simple—so simple that even a child can spread the Gospel.

> "With more than 50 percent of the world's population living in oral cultures, most with no written form of their language, [translation for oral Bible storytelling] is perfect for quickly bringing God's Word to men, women, and children in some of the world's most remote, backward places."

Oral Bible storytelling has made a profound impact in places like the war-torn Democratic Republic of the Congo. Only God's Word can bring comfort to those who have lost family, friends, and loved ones to violence and abuse. Here and elsewhere around the world, people are hearing God's Word in their languages for the first time through oral Bible storytelling. One translation field coordinator explained the effectiveness this way: "Storytelling is a strength in oral cultures. Tell a Bible story to three people, and it goes viral; fifty people will hear it in a very short time."

It just makes sense. In cultures where virtually all information is transmitted by one person speaking to another, what could be more natural than people sharing the "greatest story ever told"?

Taking Risks, Pushing Boundaries

These three simple, yet powerful strategies—partnering with the Jesus Film Project and its profound, audiovisual impact; "cluster" translation projects, creating "hotspots" of Bible access for related people groups; and empowerment of heart-language Bible storytellers in oral cultures—have allowed the Bible translation movement to accomplish an unprecedented acceleration of Bible translation for previously unreached people groups around the world.

We ventured into other new areas as well, including "crowd-sourced" translation, using the Internet. In July 2011, we began to get more and more interested in the importance of the Internet as a tool for not only accomplishing the work of Bible translation, but at the same time creating opportunities for Bible engagement—often without people realizing they were becoming engaged.

The big question for us was, "Will it work in areas where Christianity is a minority religion? Where there is poverty, no electricity, and no running water?" We also wondered, "Will anyone even participate?"

None of us knew what to expect. We tested the waters with the launch of a pilot CrowdSeed project for a language in a sensitive region in India. We were anxious, expectant, prayerful, and thankful for generous financial partners who made it possible. Ultimately, we were looking to God for the outcome.

This was one of those "new paths" God spoke to us about as we sought His direction. We were running full speed ahead with a plan that just might get God's Word in edgewise to a people group who didn't have the Gospel in their language. Project leaders hoped to engage 1,000 church volunteers to review translated Scripture from the Gospel of Luke. That level of involvement would be a mind-boggling success in any region, especially one where another major religion ruled. It was a response only God could accomplish.

By project's end, more than 3,000 eager volunteers had gathered around computer stations to participate. Participants came from every lifestyle, every age—even other faiths in some instances—young people, old people, husbands, and wives. Teenagers helped elders navigate Web-based technology, and elders shared their knowledge of Scripture with the youth. Participants came from twelve different Christian church movements; talk about breaking down silos! Others were non-Christians who came out of curiosity, interested in a project that focused on their language.

By using technology to remove issues of distance, social barriers, and political forces, Scripture was translated and feedback gathered through *virtual* community testing. More than 6,630 hours in this pilot phase were spent translating and validating seven chapters of Luke.

Success? Local church attendance grew as much as 20 percent. Pastors were thrilled. New bonds were formed as participants worked side by side, reviewing Scriptures. In addition, those involved felt a tremendous sense of ownership in the project, and life transformation is still taking place in this part of India as a result. As participants worked on God's Word, the words of Jesus worked on them, sneaking in and planting the seed of God's Truth deep in their hearts. And God is giving the increase, as Paul describes in 1 Corinthians 3:6.

Another tool that we used to accelerate the pace of translation work was VAST: Video/Audio Strategy for Translation. This new initiative proved both powerful and successful for bringing God's Word to a group of people in India who suffer from decades of discrimination, in part because of historical forces that have conspired to thrust them into poverty and crime.

The Kaylar of south India lost their lands and livelihoods during colonial rule in the nineteenth century. In order to survive, many of them turned to theft, which resulted in the Kaylar being declared a "criminal tribe." The government confined thousands of Kaylar in camps and invited a Christian organization to teach them "morality." Though such forced efforts rarely show more than marginal success, a few Kaylar were reached, forming a small base of faithful among this largely oral culture.

In 2011, with help from our partners in the Summer Institute for Linguistics, we launched a pilot program for VAST among the Kaylar. Working with Kaylar Christians, we helped translate the Jesus Film from the regional trade language into the Kaylar mother tongue. This pilot project was met with such enthusiasm by the Kaylar translators that they beat every deadline, and the production of the Kaylar version of the Jesus Film was completed in only four months—a new land-speed record! Two weeks later, at the December 2011 dedication ceremony, 500 Kaylar families received a copy of the film in their mother tongue. Each family committed to show the film to at least ten other families, giving Jesus the opportunity to "speak" to literally thousands of people who had never before heard or read a word of Scripture.

Setting Goals, Breaking Records

During my ten-plus years at this young startup operation inaugurated by Bernie May from a converted broom closet, we were able to impact Scripture translation projects for over 1,000 languages. Such a rate of work had never before been achieved in the worldwide Bible translation history. This remarkable accomplishment is a result of the grace and provision of God and the like-minded dedication of partners around the world. As I said earlier, when the body of Christ pools its talents and resources and unifies around a goal, the sky is the limit.

> "During my ten-plus years at this young startup operation inaugurated by Bernie May from a converted broom closet, we were able to impact Scripture translation projects for over 1,000 languages. Such a rate of work had never before been achieved in the worldwide Bible translation history."

These were fulfilling years for Rita and me as we watched God's Word going into places that would have been considered impossible just a short time before. Again and again, we witnessed God breaking down barriers and making a way out of no way for those willing to step forward in faith. On so many occasions, we wept with joy and amazement as we watched people hear or read God's Word in their heart language for the first time in their lives. We experienced the awe-inspiring presence of the Holy Spirit: in thatched-roof churches in Africa; in open-sky gathering places in India; beneath immense trees in South America; on windswept hillsides in China; and in our offices and meeting rooms in the United States of America.

I could not imagine being anywhere else or doing anything else. But, as you might expect by now, God had another challenge in mind for us.

Food for Thought

- In order to accomplish something that has never been done, sometimes you must try something that has never been attempted.

- Usually, no single ministry has the unique key to success; often, cooperation among ministries yields exponentially greater results.

- There is no limit to what the Word of God can do when it is planted in human hearts.

Questions to Consider

1. When you are trying something new, are you willing to make mistakes? Would it be okay if you failed?

2. Can you remember the last time someone told you a story? How did it make you feel? Did it communicate lessons or truths?

3. What is the most effective way you have learned about the Gospel? Was it through reading the Bible? Hearing it taught in church? Depicted in a movie? What made this mode so effective?

Chapter 16

BEGINNING AGAIN

I am making everything new! . . .
These words are trustworthy and true.

Revelation 21:5, NIV

I n 1998, I was sitting in the guest house of the Salvation Army in London, attending a meeting of the Forum of Bible Agencies, an international group that promotes collaboration among most of the world's Bible translation organizations. At that meeting, I met Dr. Gene Habecker, who was serving as president of American Bible Society.

Within moments of meeting, Gene and I realized that we needed to be friends. We shared many values and felt a deep sense of camaraderie. Over the next months, Rita and I enjoyed many occasions with Gene and his wife, Marylou, as our brief meeting in London developed into a sincere friendship.

Not long into our young friendship, Gene said something odd to me. "Roy," he said, "I have the sense that I won't be at ABS that many more years, and I have the further sense that you should be my replacement."

I was rather surprised to hear this. After all, at that time I was serving in my new role as president of Wycliffe, we were in the

213

process of relocating from California to Florida, God was moving powerfully, and I was in my tenth year on Wycliffe's staff and certainly not looking to change jobs.

Some years later, as I was settling in at my new role at The Seed Company, Gene made a similar comment. Though I had deep respect for Gene as a man of God and a skilled and perceptive leader, I was still resistant to any notion of seeking a different leadership role with all that was happening at The Seed Company. And yet, as I pondered Gene's words prayerfully, I couldn't escape the sense that there was something to it. I didn't know what, exactly, and I definitely lacked the certainty to say anything to any of my ministry partners at The Seed Company, but I couldn't just dismiss it.

In fact, during the decade I spent at The Seed Company, as I continued to pray over these things, I often received a sense of vision about what the future might hold for American Bible Society. Even as I got these spiritual promptings, however, I would remind myself, "But I'm the president of The Seed Company! I'm here because of God's prompting through prayer and fasting; why would He call me to American Bible Society?" Round and round the internal conversation went.

When Gene stepped down from ABS to lead a great Christian university, he urged me to contact the ABS board. I declined. I just couldn't see how the timing made any sense.

The Call That Wouldn't Go Away

Over the next few years, American Bible Society appointed two more presidents. I clearly remember that the first person chosen to succeed Gene was with me at a meeting in Germany. As we rode together in a taxi, he said to me, "Roy, I'm interim; I don't think I'm going to be leading ABS for the long term, and I think you are probably the person who should have the job."

In other words, the last two leaders of ABS have now told me that I should consider taking their jobs. Would you be getting a hint at this point? Well, I wasn't there yet.

A few more years passed, and at another meeting of ministry leaders, this time in New York City, the subsequent president of ABS—like Gene and his successor, a godly, seasoned leader—Dr. Lamar Vest, was hosting me. He turned to me and said—can you guess?—"Roy, I don't think I'm going to be leading ABS much longer; I think you ought to be the next president."

Mind you, by this time I had been at The Seed Company for about eight years, and our ministry was growing rapidly. We were seeing God's Word reaching far and wide, going into more and more new places. I could not have been any happier or more satisfied. I was not looking for another job! And yet, repeatedly, I was hearing—from the last three sitting presidents of ABS, no less—that I should consider coming there in a leadership role. And the Spirit of God was continually whispering in my ear, not allowing me to stop considering the possibility.

When God's Spirit Moves

I received a call from the board of American Bible Society toward the end of 2013. Reluctantly, I agreed to meet with them. Going into that meeting, Rita and I decided to place a fleece before the Lord, in the manner of Gideon. We decided, among other things, that the only way I would accept the leadership of ABS was if the board was unanimous in its invitation. You see, I know a little something about boards of directors, and the way I figured it, requiring a unanimous vote on my presidency was equal to a quick ticket out of the meeting.

As Rita and I walked into the meeting room with the ABS board, we realized they had been worshipping together. As that knowledge was sinking in, they informed me that they had just unanimously elected me to be the next CEO of American Bible Society.

Rita and I looked at each other. I suppose we shouldn't have been surprised, considering all the times we had seen God's dramatic answers to prayer. But we also knew that we now had to go back to The Seed Company and inform our dear friends and ministry partners that God had decided to move me into the leadership of American Bible Society.

Inheriting an Honored Legacy

American Bible Society was founded in 1816 in New York City. Its first president, Elias Boudinot, had previously served as an advisor to George Washington during the Revolutionary War. He was the first director of the US Mint, a three-term congressman, and had been president of the Fourth Continental Congress.

The first chief justice of the Supreme Court, John Jay, was the second ABS president. Other early leaders of American Bible Society included John Quincy Adams, the sixth president of the US, and Francis Scott Key, who wrote the national anthem. To say that ABS has a distinguished history would be the understatement of the decade.

As I moved into my new role, I was keenly aware of that history and of the immense legacy it represented. ABS had produced its first Bible translation in 1818, just two years after its founding: providing Scripture for the Lenape, a Native American tribe from the Delaware region. In 1829, the leaders of this thirteen-year-old ministry determined to offer Bibles to every poor family in America. Previously their Bible distribution had numbered in the hundreds, but with this bold commitment nearly 600,000 Bibles were given out in the next few years. This was also the first organization to provide Bibles for the military in time of war, producing pocket-sized Bibles that Civil War soldiers carried into battle and elsewhere.

But one of the reasons I had come to ABS was to investigate new directions. Without losing an ounce of respect for the organization's cherished past, I was charged

> "To its everlasting credit, the board of ABS recognized, not only that new directions were needed in order to keep the organization relevant and positioned for growth, but also that its very deep roots in tradition could, if not carefully monitored, constitute a threat to those very new initiatives that offered the best chance for progress."

with charting new directions for its future. And as you can imagine, changing directions can be challenging for an institution with the type of deep tradition possessed by American Bible Society.

To its everlasting credit, the board of ABS recognized, not only that new directions were needed in order to keep the organization relevant and positioned for growth, but also that its very deep roots in tradition could, if not carefully monitored, constitute a threat to those very new initiatives that offered the best chance for progress. The board proved this in a powerful way when it voted, of its own accord, to impose term limits on board service—for the first time in the organization's almost two hundred-year history.

To get an idea of what an immense step that was, it might help you to know, for example, that Ruth Stafford Peale, the wife of Norman Vincent Peale, served the board of American Bible Society for fifty years—half a century! Also, her daughter, Elizabeth Peale Allen, was on the board that hired me. And yet, recognizing that the leadership model had to change, she, along with her fellow servant-leaders, chose to give up an activity that they personally cherished in order to promote the betterment of this mission. More than continuing to sit on the governing board of an institution to which they have given years of their lives, they wanted ABS to have decades more in which to do the work for which it was founded: taking the Word of God to the peoples of the world in their own languages.

New Directions

One of the first initiatives we undertook was to relocate the Society's headquarters from New York to Philadelphia. Let that sink in for a moment: ABS had been in New York for 199 years, since its founding in 1816. Board members—like Elizabeth Peale Allen—with deep New York roots and decades of service to ABS realized, as I did, that in order to shift the emphasis of the organization in the ways necessary to insure future success, we needed to relocate to a place less cost-prohibitive than downtown Manhattan. Similar to the situation Wycliffe had in California in the late 1990s, ABS was finding it increasingly difficult to attract talented young staffers, given the expense of living in New York City.

But it wasn't an easy decision. Imagine the emotion aroused by contemplating leaving a place where an organization has been since its founding—almost two hundred years ago. And yet the ABS board, placing the welfare of the mission above personal preference, voted to sell the property at 1865 Broadway and move to our present location at 401 Market Street in downtown Philadelphia, across from the Liberty Bell.

We've begun changing more than our location, too. As we renew our mission in the City of Brotherly Love, we are keenly aware of the relationship of the Bible to not only our national liberty, but also to the freedom of all humankind. We have announced plans to open the Faith and Liberty Discovery Center, as described in an earlier chapter. We want to offer visitors to historic Philadelphia a chance to engage with the Bible and its place in American history. Using state-of-the-art interactive technology, we intend to present the life-changing story of the Bible in a way that engages the imaginations and hearts of modern Americans. By doing this, we expect to advance the transformation of American culture, as God's Word speaks afresh to current and future generations.

> "As we renew our mission in the City of Brotherly Love, we are keenly aware of the relationship of the Bible to not only our national liberty, but also to the freedom of all humankind."

In fact, we propose to increase Bible engagement among Americans from its present level of less than 50 million actively engaged to 100 million; we intend to do this in the next ten years. Can you imagine the transformational impact it will have on our nation when the number of our citizens who are actively engaged with the Bible is doubled? With an estimated 400,000 people visiting our Faith and Liberty Discovery Center every year, and more online, we can take giant steps toward promoting this level of Bible engagement. God's Word is still powerful and active, and He will help us reach this goal if we are willing to step out boldly in faith.

". . . we propose to increase Bible engagement among Americans from its present level of less than 50 million actively engaged to 100 million; we intend to do this in the next ten years. By 2025, with God's help and the continued faithful support of our ministry partners, we anticipate that every person on the planet will be able to read or hear the Bible in his or her heart language."

We are also moving forward to increase the acceleration in Bible translation for the remaining Bible-less people groups of the world. As I previously described, the Digital Bible Library is revolutionizing the availability of the Bible as technology continues to break down barriers all across the world. Partnering with other ministry groups—including translation organizations, publishers, software developers, and outreach groups—

ABS participation in the illumiNations initiative is a major part of our strategy to get the Bible into more than 1,600 remaining heart languages where it does not presently exist. By 2025, with God's help and the continued faithful support of our ministry partners, we anticipate that every person on the planet will be able to read or hear the Bible in his or her heart language.

And, as God's Word goes into the hurting places in the world, ABS anticipates an unprecedented opportunity to aid in "the healing of nations." Where the trauma of war, disease, abuse, neglect, and famine now hold sway, we will bring the hope of Scripture, restoring people to the life their Creator intended for them. God's Word must be opened for the wounded heart. As a woman told us after coming to one of our Trauma Healing Workshops in West Africa, "When I came, I preferred death to life. But after these two weeks of the seminar, I feel relieved, and I have hope for the future." By training facilitators and offering Bible-based resources, we are helping to provide essential hope where it is needed most.

> "Where the trauma of war, disease, abuse, neglect, and famine now hold sway, we will bring the hope of Scripture, restoring people to the life their Creator intended for them. God's Word must be opened for the wounded heart."

Finishing the Task

It is a thrilling time to be involved in the Bible movement. Today, the church has the technology, the resources, the expertise, and the dedicated people to accomplish things we could barely imagine just a decade ago. God is supplying our needs and also supplying the vision we will require in order to continue to meet the needs of the future.

As I reflect on these past decades, I am continually astounded at the ways God's grace has enabled me to participate in His work in the world. Almost nothing in my youth or upbringing could have prepared me for the ways God has touched my life—rescuing it, preserving it, enriching it, and directing it along the path He has appointed for me. I have more to be grateful for than I could ever express in words.

> "If you will look deeply into your own heart, you will see that God has blessed you with unique abilities and dreams. You, too, are part of His plan to redeem a lost and hurting world. You have a part, an essential contribution to make."

And so do you! If you will look deeply into your own heart, you will see that God has blessed you with unique abilities and dreams. You, too, are part of His plan to redeem a lost and hurting world. You have a part, an essential contribution to make.

Just as God was able to take my meager talents and shape them to His will, He can use you to carry out His purposes in your community, your workplace, your home. You may feel like an unlikely candidate for the work of God, but I can assure you that there was never a more unlikely candidate than me.

In fact, I think God specializes in using the unlikely to achieve the unstoppable. That has been my experience during these years, as I have watched His Word go into some of the unlikeliest places on earth. I want to continue to participate with Him. I believe that as long as we walk in faith and in step with God, the future is bright, the possibilities are endless, and the next steps are critical.

> "... God specializes in using the unlikely to achieve the unstoppable."

The work doesn't end until the whole world hears. Jesus said, "And this Good News about the Kingdom will be preached through all the world" (Matthew 24:14, GNT). God confirms the word of His Son when He said, through His prophet, "But the earth will be as full of the knowledge of the LORD's glory as the seas are full of water" (Habakkuk 2:14, GNT).

Food for Thought

- God sees possibilities for our lives that we cannot imagine.

- When human hearts are deeply committed to change, anything is possible.

- The challenges we face are never greater than God's ability to accomplish His will.

Questions to Consider

1. Have you ever witnessed or participated in a major change in an organization? What were the greatest challenges you faced? What were the rewards for making the necessary changes?

2. Why do you think our sense of timing is often different from God's? How can we be more sensitive to God's leading in such times?

3. Why do you think so many Americans are "Bible skeptics"? What do you consider as the three greatest barriers to Bible engagement in our country today?

CONCLUSION

YOUR TURN

N ow it's not my story anymore; it's yours—and, of course, God's. How will He empower you to connect with Him in the Bible and help others do the same? How will your encounter with God in Scripture change your life and the lives around you?

We live in a critical time for our communities, our nation, and the world. People need the transforming Word of God like never before, but all too often the Bible is met with disdain and dismissal. In home after home, in school after school, they're being

> "How will your encounter with God in Scripture change your life and the lives around you?"

shelved instead of studied. We have the solution to the world's most pressing problems, but it's being left in the library while the problems intensify.

How will you meet the current crisis?

The challenges of this time call for faithfulness and boldness. We must be faithful to the Lord, who is faithful to us. And we must spring to life with bold innovation, applying new methods, new technologies, to the work of sharing God's Word.

But faithfulness starts first, here in our own hearts. Is the Bible a part of your everyday life? I'm talking about more than a few verses casually read and quickly forgotten. Are you allowing God's Word to engage your heart and mind on a regular basis? Are you allowing the Word of God to make you more and more like the Son of God? The God who made you and who sustains your life from moment to moment longs to speak to you. Will you listen? Are you willing to act on what He tells you? Are you willing to talk about the Bible with others—not just in a church class or small group, but in everyday life? If God is transforming you through Scripture, your family and friends might like to know.

> "Are you allowing God's Word to engage your heart and mind on a regular basis? Are you allowing the Word of God to make you more and more like the Son of God?"

And this is where the bold work of the Bible movement begins. Transforming our nation has to start with individual lives—beginning with each of us. Going where hope meets hurt. The ministry of trauma healing may be sparked to life in your community. And while the work of Bible translation continues around the globe, you—in your life—may be right now, the best translation your friends are going to get.

226

For all the changes of our world, one thing will never change: God's Word continues to bring life. His Gospel longs to be unlocked, opening hope in lives across the globe. And it may well be that the key is sitting in your pocket—if you'll reach deep . . . remembering His faithfulness . . . praying for what is possible if we all give unreservedly to see His Word released to people across the globe.

"... you—in your life— may be right now, the best translation your friends are going to get."

When I look back across the decades to that terrified and hopeless teenager, it still brings tears to my eyes. In that moment, I could see no further than the shadow of a locked Mexican prison cell. But the truth is, God set me free.

And I'm convinced: He's not done yet.